PRAISE FOR *HACKING QUESTIONS*

"Connie will push your thinking and equip you with invaluable questioning strategies that all K–12 teachers need to use! She has helped me become more intentional when questioning my students and the results have been remarkable. The best part is that my students are now modeling Connie's techniques when they question each other!"

— Kristy Babyak, Elementary Teacher

"Look out, Socrates! Here comes Connie Hamilton, the newest innovator of questionology! Connie Hamilton is leading teachers to create a higher level of learning through questioning techniques that can only be compared to the Golden Age."

— Marcia Gutiérrez, High School Educator

"Connie has the unique ability to know how to support teachers with the knowledge and confidence to understand their roles when asking questions to increase student thinking and engagement. She is an amazing presenter. You can take your learning immediately into the classroom!"

— Simone Margraf, Curriculum/Instruction/MTSS District Coordinator/K–8 Instructional Coach

"Connie Hamilton is a highly skilled facilitator who provides teachers with the opportunity to reflect on their questioning and bring clarity to what is essential in student learning. She consciously shapes professional development with an inquiry approach. It is evident that she is a true champion for student and teacher success!"

— Stephanie O'C̶ ̶ ̶ Middle School Principal

"In a very short amount of tin̶ ̶ ̶ ̶ ̶ ̶ ̶ ̶ ̶ ̶ ̶ my eyes to the art of questioning. C̶ ̶ ̶ ̶ ̶ ̶ ̶ ̶ ̶ ̶ ̶ nore from my students by questioni̶ ̶ ̶ ̶ ̶ ̶ ̶ ̶ ̶ ̶ and inviting to the students in order to deepen tṉ̶ ̶ ̶ ̶ ̶ I feel

fortunate to have had the training and welcome any further professional development from such a guru of questioning."

—DEBBIE PAPPAS, ELEMENTARY MATH TEACHER

"Our teachers have the wonderful opportunity to learn along with Connie. She has a wealth of knowledge around teaching and learning. Connie is a masterful coach, facilitator and presenter. She crafts questions for teachers to have deep reflection around their practice. Connie's work provides teachers with effective techniques they can implement right away to strengthen the purpose of their lessons."

— CHERYL THOMAS, ELEMENTARY PRINCIPAL

"Connie is an incredible driver of change in our focus on classroom questioning as a best practice instructional strategy. Her support in our district has rebuilt classroom questioning into its most efficient and effective form to date. I've learned so much from Connie in the realm of classroom questioning, best practices, and all things related to excellent teaching."

— TROY VANDERLAAN, MIDDLE SCHOOL ADMINISTRATOR

"The way Connie presented questioning and how she connected it helped me to better understand student learning. The workshops applied to all grade levels and were interactive. I continue to use her models with my students daily."

— MICHELLE MACI, HIGH SCHOOL TEACHER

HACKING QUESTIONS

HACKING QUESTIONS

11 ANSWERS
THAT CREATE
A CULTURE OF
INQUIRY IN YOUR
CLASSROOM

HACK™
Learning
SERIES

Connie
Hamilton

Hacking Questions
© 2019 by Times 10 Publications

These books are available at special discounts when purchased in quantity for use as premiums, promotions, fundraising, and educational use. For inquiries and details, contact us at 10publications.com.

Published by Times 10
Highland Heights, OH
10publications.com

Cover Design by Steven Plummer
Interior Design by Steven Plummer
Editing by Carrie White-Parrish
Proofreading by Jennifer Jas

Library of Congress Cataloging-in-Publication Data is available.
ISBN: 978-1-948212-14-4
First Printing: April, 2019
Second Printing: March, 2020
Third Printing: May, 2021

A Special Note of Thanks and Love to:

Paul, Trey, Luke, and Allie
Q: Who are you?
A: Hamilton!

Starr Sackstein
Q: How did we get here?
A: Friendship.

Laura Pitari
Q: Who knew?
A: You did.

TABLE OF CONTENTS

INTRODUCTION
QUESTIONING LEADS TO GROWTH

*The art and science of asking questions
is the source of all knowledge.*
— Thomas Berger, Author of *Little Big Man*

S O MANY FACTORS come into play when you're posing questions, because inquiry is more complex than just crafting perfect questions. These factors include: In what ways are you intentional with how you ask questions in your classroom? Do you attend to verbs? Are you mindful of timing? Do you follow a sequence? What types of questions do you ask? How are learners engaged? Who is doing the thinking?

These topics are important because they affect not only the way you come across, but also the answers you'll receive.

This book focuses primarily on the delivery of questions. I highlight questioning as a verb, to push your thinking about how and why you ask questions. In my experience working with teachers, and as a teacher myself, I have picked up strategies that impact the conditions and reactions to questions. Some of these strategies are tweaks tied to existing tools in most every teacher's toolbox. Others might challenge the assumptions you have made for years. Whether we are giving old practices a fresh perspective or undoing old habits, we will look at the purpose of your decisions around questioning. Teachers are intentional about most of their instructional choices, but questioning is sometimes taken for granted. The eleven strategies in this book will help you focus on what, when, why, and how questions are flying in your classroom.

How did I come up with these strategies? I have experienced the pure joy of working intimately with hundreds of teachers in small-group settings while writing *Hacking Questions*. These groups are Collaboration and Instructional Feedback Teams, or CIFTs, and consist of four to six teachers who meet multiple times a year to watch one another teach. Each teacher on the team hosts a minimum of once every year. On a CIFT day, the team meets for approximately half a day, broken into three parts:

1. **Prebrief:** The host teacher describes the lesson and responds to questions about how they developed the lesson. We dig deeply into how decisions were made, the intent of those decisions, and the unknowns going into the lesson. Questions we look at might include:

   • What is the purpose of having a student from each team share the group's conclusions?

- What is the most important part of the lesson?

- How long is too long/short for your mini lesson?

- How will you close the lesson?

- What evidence will you have at the end of the lesson that each student has met the learning target for today?

- What questions do you have prepared?

- How will you support students who struggle?

- What criteria will you use to determine whether you should move on?

- What will you think about as you're listening to students have discussions?

- What will your role be during student collaboration time?

Many of these reflective questions reveal intentionality. Hearing the host's response to these details helps the team gather data to support the teacher in the journey for continuous learning and growth.

The prebrief is essential to the process. In addition to revealing the host teacher's lesson purpose, it models questioning. Since everyone has sat in what has been called "the hot seat" in a CIFT, everyone has an appreciation for the depth of thought—or sometimes lack thereof—put into the actions that take place during the course of the lesson.

Observers reflect on their own classrooms, but

also benefit from hearing the host's thought process as they travel toward a decision. Oftentimes, we hear what sounds like music to our ears when the host explains why they made a decision, but equally as important, why they dismissed a different decision.

2. **Observation:** When the host teaches the class, the host asks the rest of the CIFT team to collect the requested data. This can be anything from the timing of the lesson to charting the path the teacher takes during collaborative learning. And—of course—we collect data on questioning techniques. How many questions are asked? Are they open- or closed-ended questions? What levels are the questions? How much thinking time are students allowed before they must respond to the questions? The rest of the team is in charge of collecting data based on what the host wants to review.

3. **Debrief:** After the lesson, everyone privately reflects and prepares feedback. After the host identifies what went well, and what they would change if they could, they request specific feedback on the lesson. Each CIFT member shares the collected data and provides "glows and grows." Glows are observations that note particular areas of strength and specific portions of the lesson that were successful. Grows are suggestions for growth. Growth does not always mean improvement, but may include suggestions for different ways of accomplishing the same outcome. The more tools we can add to our instructional toolbox, the better

prepared we are for anything that comes our way in the learning process.

I have taken part in over three hundred CIFT sessions in the past two years, and have observed preschool to high school Advanced Placement classes in dozens of subject areas. This big picture has given me the opportunity to see patterns in planning, teaching, noticing, and reflecting.

It is this perspective from which I framed the eleven Hacks in this book. I identified the most universal and successful answers to problems that surface over and over again in classrooms across multiple contents and grade levels, and used them to build what I believe to be an overview of the idea of questions in the classroom. This is not a rulebook for questioning in the sense that a strategy is right or wrong, though. You will find that each Hack addresses the same process: figuring out a student's intention and purpose, and then building questions around it. We'll look at the student's position, and how knowing that can help you sort through the thousands of decisions you make every day. You'll see guides for learning to base your in-the-moment decisions on a level of purpose. I'll teach you to identify how, when, and why you should ask questions, and how that deserves just as much attention as what the question is.

I'll also provide examples to illustrate each of the Hacks. Remember that these illustrations are models intended to spark your thinking rather than offer an exclusive list. As with any instructional strategy, there are always exceptions. The Hacks are not laws; they are solutions to common problems that great teachers will undoubtedly recognize from their own classrooms.

While each Hack stands alone, it is also interwoven with the others. As you read each chapter, it might spur other wonderings or thoughts about questioning. For example, it would be incomplete to talk about how to facilitate student collaboration without referencing the teacher's role during that time. In this book, those strategies are two different Hacks that build upon one another. If you find a Hack of interest and want to go deeper, keep reading. There are opportunities to connect throughout the chapters.

YOU WILL FIND THIS MAGNIFYING GLASS THROUGHOUT THE TEXT.

You will find this magnifying glass throughout the text. The image serves as a suggestion to take a closer and deeper look at the message. In the lens, you'll find words of caution, words of wisdom, and teacher tips. Many of the resources referenced in the Hacks are also available in high resolution and can be downloaded at HackingQuestions.com.

HACK 1

ASSUME ALL HANDS ARE UP

EXPECT THAT EVERY STUDENT WILL ENGAGE

Tell me and I forget. Show me and I remember.
Involve me and I understand.

— CHINESE PROVERB

THE PROBLEM: TEACHERS SOLICIT
ENGAGEMENT THROUGH HAND RAISING

A GREAT DEBATE EXISTS between whether or not teachers should cold-call students or allow them to volunteer to respond. Arguments in favor of cold-calling suggest that the element of surprise keeps students on their toes. Those opposed to this practice, however, are sensitive to the emotional side of how students feel when they're called on and don't know the answer. Let's explore the most common results of encouraging hand raising in the classroom.

After a teacher asks a question to a class, one of three things usually happens:

1. A single hand shoots up and the teacher quickly calls on that student.

2. Several students raise their hands and the teacher either tries to vary who to select, or chooses the student most likely to respond accurately.

3. Crickets.

In the first example, where a star pupil straightens an elbow toward the ceiling, we tend to see the same hands up over and over again. This results in a small group of learners monopolizing the interactions. But teachers often feel guilty for *not* calling on those eager beavers who always seem willing to learn and are consistently engaged. They may sigh loudly when the teacher doesn't select them to share, and flop down their hands in disappointment.

The problem is, without intentional strategies for addressing how to select volunteers, and making sure that you're selecting from the entire group, a classroom can change from a learning group of twenty-eight to a smaller group of eight, with twenty silent observers.

At other times, a teacher floats a question to the class and a sea of waving hands shoots up in the air. Now the issue is *whom* to choose. One thought is to select the student who does not usually participate. The notion is that rewarding the effort to join the learning will carry over to future lessons and increase that student's willingness to take a risk. Yet what we are unintentionally validating is that the student can choose when to engage. Hand up: Yes, I want to share. Hand down: Leave me out of the learning. Commonly, teachers will select three or more students to share their thinking with the class, even if twenty hands are in the air. While this increases the percentage of active, engaged brains, we are still only hitting the 10-percent mark when it comes to getting students involved.

Then there is the dreaded silence. It can be deafening. If no students respond, three top reactions include:

1. Catching students off guard by calling a name in hopes that a student will offer a thought.

2. The Bueller response begging for "anyone?...anyone?" to break the silence.

Look at it this way: If it is worth pausing to ask one student, isn't it worth asking them all?

3. Or worst of all, we end up answering our own question.

The assumption, when there's no response, is that the question is too difficult, or maybe was unclear. We get inside our own heads and start wondering how in the world they could possibly not understand. Then we automatically jump into reteaching mode. You have just called on your most knowledgeable student: YOU!

When your questioning purpose is to check for understanding before moving on with the lesson, a sampling of students is likely insufficient data. Generalizing that the whole class "gets it" based on the response of a select few is a recipe for disaster. Triggering each and every student to provide evidence that they are learning along the way will provide you with a better indication of what your next steps should be. Too often, teachers wait until the end of the lesson—or worse, the end of the unit—to assess student comprehension. Look at it this way: If it is worth pausing to ask one student, isn't it worth asking them all?

What all of these circumstances have in common is that the question is posed for the purpose of getting an answer so the lesson can move on. By soliciting volunteers and getting a quick answer from a small sample of students, teachers feel validated that the lesson is going well, and they continue forward. This process is flawed. As we've seen, this isn't a true sampling of the entire classroom. Plus, the strategy of requiring students to raise their hands to respond to a question sends a message that a student should have a prepared and accurate reply *before* speaking. This discourages full engagement and focuses attention on the students who already know the answer, allowing confused students to get lost along the way. And you won't know it until it is too late.

We have to find a more efficient, more effective way of assessing the entire class's understanding of a lesson, and to do that we need to learn to present questions in a different way.

THE HACK: ASSUME ALL HANDS ARE UP

Rather than taking a side on the cold-calling debate, adopt the mindset that every learner can and should engage in thinking. This includes the whole class, small groups, and independent structures for instruction. Would you ever pose the question, "Who chooses to learn today?" then accept only five hands? No! Occasionally, hearing one voice at a time might be your method of choice, but it should not be your default strategy to call on single students to confirm that the whole class understands.

The hacky part of this practice is not the actual protocols. Think-Pair-Share, hold up visuals, movement, and similar strategies are tried-and-true practices that educators have been using for decades. No, the message for this Hack is that we need to think about all students interacting as the norm, not the exception. Plan your lessons with the intention of finding logical points for pauses. Then assume all students are as ready and eager to participate as Hermione Granger, waving their hands in the air in the hopes of showing off their studious personas. Prepare an activity that gives dignity to all students by creating the opportunity for 100 percent of them to be "chosen."

Disengagement is the enemy of learning. We unintentionally create the conditions for disengagement when we allow students to keep their hands down. Assuming that all hands are up creates a culture in the classroom that is inviting to the entire population. You will send the consistent message to your learners that you expect everyone to join the journey to success. No one is singled out ... and no one is *left* out.

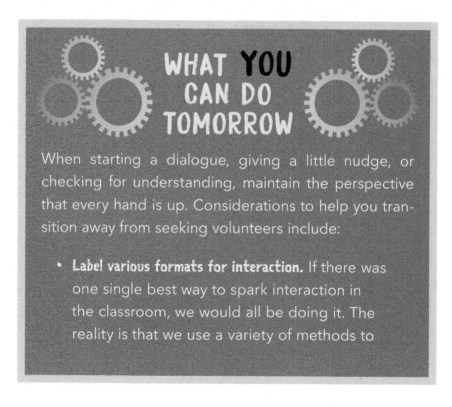

WHAT YOU CAN DO TOMORROW

When starting a dialogue, giving a little nudge, or checking for understanding, maintain the perspective that every hand is up. Considerations to help you transition away from seeking volunteers include:

- **Label various formats for interaction.** If there was one single best way to spark interaction in the classroom, we would all be doing it. The reality is that we use a variety of methods to engage students. Sometimes we accept students responding freely, and sometimes we want them to hold off until they're prompted to engage. Teach students a few protocols for responding so that they know what to expect, and then access these triggers by name. Here are a few common formats:

- **Blurt time.** Invite students to give their thoughts as they come to mind without needing permission to share. Blurting is ideal for times when the class is recalling information to activate prior knowledge, or brainstorming ideas. The benefit of blurt time, sometimes called "popcorn response," is that attention isn't focused on an individual student. It is typically fast and efficient, and it raises the energy level of the entire class. Students also learn the skill of listening for the lull to be sure their voices are heard. During blurt time, discussion is usually reserved until all the ideas are on the table. Then they can be processed as a collective whole. During discussion, common ideas can be lumped together, and misconceptions can either be explored or noted by the teacher to debunk in the near future.

- **Take volunteers.** This Hack is not about abolishing hand raising, but about being more intentional with how it is used. At times, you'll need a volunteer, including when you're demonstrating a point or completing a job such as passing out materials. Asking students who can share specific experiences is another example of when you would tell students you are going to solicit volunteers. If you launch with, "I'd like a volunteer to," you will reinforce that hand raising is not the norm in your classroom.

- **All hands up.** Communicate to students that you assume they always have their hands up. When you make *all hands up time* different from *blurt time*, for example, you prevent potential management issues with students shouting out answers when you are planning a quiet think time. When students are warned in advance that it's an all hands up portion of the lesson, they know the expectation is that all will be engaged in active thinking and learning—and waiting their turn. Then you can randomly select anyone, or use a strategy to have all students responding. One such strategy

is Stop and Jot, where students use a
journal, whiteboard, or laptop to write
down key points they are learning and
document any questions they have.

- **Take time for talk.** Instead of posing a question to the entire class and asking one student to respond, pose a question to the entire class and allow the entire class to respond in partners. Create shoulder or elbow partners in your class. Identify an A and B partner. Some teachers of younger students have pairings like peanut butter and jelly partners. Having A/B partners also allows you to facilitate who asks and who responds, mixing it up to give each partner equal talk time.

- **Change stems before questions are posed to the whole class.** How you position a question can influence the comfort level students have in contributing their thoughts. Questions that assume that students are processing their new learning can make all the difference. Consider opening a class discussion with, "What are you wondering about?" or "How are you making sense of this?" These questions are more metacognitive, and invite students to think about their thinking around the content without expecting that they have already processed it. Instead of prefacing a question with, "Who knows …" try beginning with "Who can start us off in thinking about …" Then let the conversation flow naturally. Discourage students from raising their hands to contribute to the conversation, and manage the flow by using accountable talk stems (see Hack 7: Make Yourself Invisible).

- **Use equity sticks or randomization selection.** Use a simple jar of popsicle sticks to keep students from feeling like you are picking on them or avoiding them. Put each student's name on a stick. Secondary teachers, either keep a jar for each hour or assign numbers to each student and reuse the same jar each class period. Start with all of the sticks in a paper cup inside the jar. After you choose a name or number from the jar, instead of removing the stick from the jar altogether, just place it outside of the cup. This will help you keep track of students who have been called on without making it obvious. If you want to allow for students to be called on more than once, remove or ignore the small paper cup. Digital apps such as Pick Me and Random Picker can provide the same result as the jar-and-stick option.

- **Arrange your room so students can see one another.** The way the seating is set up in your classroom sends an immediate message about the expectations. It is polite to make eye contact with the person who is talking. If your classroom is set up in rows facing the front of the class, you're implying that the teacher is the center of the discussion. If your goal is for students to bounce ideas off one another and engage in conversation, make sure that they don't have to turn around to look at the speaker. Consider the three room arrangements in Image 1.1. Each of these designs equalizes the opportunity to give attention to everyone, and keeps the teacher away from center stage. When students can see their peers, they are more likely to be active in the lesson.

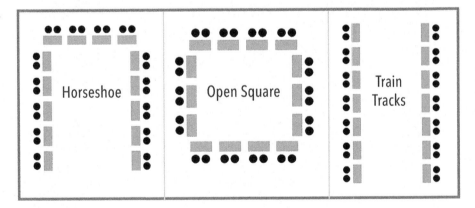

Image 1.1

A BLUEPRINT FOR FULL IMPLEMENTATION

Step 1: Explore the perfect spot for engagement.

Before you implement an all hands up, think about when it best fits in your lesson. Oftentimes, students are not invited to visibly engage until the end of a lesson, video, or lengthy text. Look within longer chunks of time to find a natural stopping spot to be sure students are cognitively engaged. Waiting until the end to find out that students were confused or tuned out is too late.

At no time should students be asked to sit and listen for longer than ten minutes. For younger students, the time limit should be even less. If the lesson you have planned for the day is heavy on establishing surface-level knowledge, identify points where you can stop and allow students to process. Think of their working memory like a water pitcher, where the water is the information you are sharing with them. Once the pitcher is full, it either needs to leak water out, or be set aside for storage. It will overflow if you pour in additional water too quickly. It won't be retained.

The answer is to let them pour the information into another container by giving them time to process the content through cognitive engagement. In this case, the exchange is from short-term to long-term memory. They move the learning from working memory (think of this as temporary) to a place where they can retrieve it later, by giving it meaning or making connections to information they already know. Once they transfer the "water" to a different part of the brain, the working memory is ready to receive new information.

Design your lesson to allow these pauses—including all hands up—*during* discussions, rather than at the end of class.

Step 2: Craft your question(s) in advance.

In order to be clear and targeted, work out the semantics around how you will pose a question related to the content. Think about how to word the question so it is concise, and you will reduce confusion for students—which is important if you're assuming that all hands are up, and all students are ready to answer. Being thoughtful with your question in advance will also maximize your instructional time and reduce the wasted time involved in rephrasing.

Step 3: Choose a strategy that assumes all hands are up and permits every student to respond.

Now that you have a placeholder and questions ready for an all hands up, it's time to choose a strategy. Consider several factors when selecting the best fit for your time slot. Here are guiding questions to ask yourself when mining protocols:

- How many students will be actively thinking?

- Do I need tangible evidence (like paper or video)?

- How quickly do I need the information?

- How much time do I have for the all hands up?

- How long have students been sitting?

- What phase of the lesson are we in (activating prior knowledge, applying, or reflecting)?

- Will students need to access their thinking later?

- What is the purpose of the all hands up (engagement, note-taking, brainstorming)?

- What materials are necessary for the protocol? Are they available?

- How complex is the protocol? Am I looking for something quick or a protocol that will assist them in processing their thinking?

- How many questions do I have?

- Is the protocol familiar or do I have to teach it?

Knowing the answers in advance will help you craft your protocol to best suit the students, and build the best success with your all hands up session.

Step 4: Gather feedback about engagement.

There is no need to keep your goal of having all hands up a secret from students. When trying a new strategy in your classroom, remember that it might not work perfectly the first time. Instead of throwing it out, invite students to identify what worked and what you could do to refine the process. This type of reflection invites metacognitive thinking. Bonus: You can model how to seek feedback for the purpose of continuing to grow *while* problem-solving in your classroom. Try these questions to gather data:

CAUTION: DON'T BE HYPOCRITICAL BY REVERTING BACK TO CALLING ON ONE STUDENT AT A TIME. BUT BE SURE YOU ARE USING AN ALL HANDS UP PROCESS TO GATHER DATA ON HOW WELL YOU'RE MEETING YOUR GOAL OF ACTIVATING THE THINKING OF ALL LEARNERS.

- What activities did you participate in today that caused you to think about your learning goal?

- How did _____ (label the thinking activity) help you meet our learning target?

- How were you able to practice your new learning today?

- What will you remember about today's lesson?

- Were there any portions of the lesson when you felt more or less included?

OVERCOMING PUSHBACK

As you move toward designing lessons that include all hands up, rebuttals might surface. Consider a deeper look at the argument. Calling on one student at a time still is not the best option in most cases.

Calling on a student who is not listening is one way to get the student's attention. This is a direct violation of Hack 11: Create a Safe Zone. If you know the student is not paying attention and you call her out by asking a question like, "Isabelle, what do you think about what Sylvia just said?" you have a mismatch in the question and its purpose. You are using a discussion prompt to address a management or behavior issue. The short-term reaction might be a sudden jerk to attention, which is the result you are seeking. Isabelle is going to have to admit that she wasn't paying attention, or you are going to battle an "I don't know" (IDK) response.

The deeper implication of calling on a student to answer a question you know darn well she is not prepared to answer is that you break down trust and reduce the rapport you have with her. You gain the perception of engagement, but only through the threat of humiliation. Instead of asking her to respond to another student's answer, try matching the question to the purpose.

"Isabelle, did you hear what Sylvia just said, or would you like her to repeat it?" This question addresses the assumption that Isabelle wasn't listening, respects her dignity, and holds her accountable for re-engaging in the discussion without triggering a defense mechanism. This type of question is a forced choice. Options are provided as possible answers to limit the response, and either answer has a natural follow-up. If Isabelle says she heard Sylvia's comment, then you can ask her to respond. If she would like Sylvia to repeat the comment, then Isabelle is more likely to be attentive and rejoin the learning, which is the goal.

Sometimes I want to hear multiple students' responses. Before hearing one response at a time, give students the opportunity to craft their narratives and even practice in a brief partner talk. This will make for more articulate and complete responses. When you have multiple students share, "airplane stacking" can save time. Airplane stacking is a strategy where you identify the students who will share all at once before the first student gives his or her thinking. Much like an air traffic controller identifies what plane will take off first, second, and third, the teacher chooses students to share in order. Instead of stopping after each response to choose another perspective, select them all up front. Students who struggle with speaking in a group or have language barriers can benefit from being third or fourth in the lineup. If they are stumped when it is their turn to speak, they now have the option to agree/disagree or paraphrase what someone else said.

If I assume they are willing to respond and they do not know the answer, we are in another pickle. Remember, it is not always about students knowing the answer. We want them to turn on their brains and think, not simply regurgitate correct answers. It is okay for students to not know the answer. Just set an expectation that everyone is expected to seek understanding and new learning. Hack 2: Kick the IDK Bucket, is dedicated to providing solutions for when students give "I don't know" responses.

Some kids are painfully shy and speaking in front of the class causes anxiety. Here is where knowing the root cause for the IDK is helpful. This situation is less about the learning and more about the social and emotional impacts. Therefore, your action should match the student's need. In this case, break the rule of thumb regarding spoon-feeding and affirming answers. Your goal is to orchestrate a successful interaction between the reticent student and the class. Instead of surprising this student with a cold-call, offer a Turn and Ask for the class to be that student's partner.

During your interaction with them, give positive reinforcement around their response, then request that they share with the class. The key is to not change up the question. The student is literally repeating the response given to you in the one-on-one exchange to the whole group. If the student is not ready for the whole group, create a foursome and ask the student to share in a small group, but one that includes peers. Then, after they've experienced positive responses from peers, ask again for them to share with the whole class. If the student still is not comfortable, one of the peer group members can paraphrase what the reserved student said. Over time, you will see an increase in the student's willingness to share as the student experiences safe interactions with open and accepting responses from the class.

Posing questions with short responses is another way to create an atmosphere where all students are expected to participate, yet you are honoring the dignity of more bashful learners as well. Slowly increase the students' stage time to help them gain more comfort in their speaking. Some might suggest alternatives to public speaking, like allowing students to use writing, video, or other more private options. These alternatives to class participation give you an opportunity to see and hear a student's thoughts. They do very little, however, to support the life skill of being an effective communicator. When you can separate content learning from social skills, you will avoid scaffolding the wrong need. Shy students don't necessarily need strategies to help them with content. Many times, the barrier is their fear of talking in front of peers. A match of interventions to the problem will lead to building their efficacy. This helps them become more confident and shows what they already know.

THE HACK IN ACTION

In her classroom, fifth-grade teacher Mrs. Michelle Perkins from Central Elementary School uses a variety of ways for students to engage in questions without hand raising at all—though the methods do assume that all students are engaged all the time. When she's teaching the Question-Answer Relationships (QAR) tool, as shared in Hack 6: Fill Your Back Pocket, Mrs. Perkins uses five intentional strategies to engage all learners, and one more when she sees the need.

When she shared the outline of the lesson with her CIFT and me, she specifically noted that she plans portions of her lessons when students will be using Clock Partners, Choral Response, Random Poll, KleenSlates, and Think-Pair-Share. During each of these interactions, 100 percent of the students were expected to be actively engaged in processing their learning. By pausing frequently to allow students to engage in thinking and talking protocols, she gave her students the chance to learn at their own rate and get the support they needed as they considered her thoughtful questions.

When Mrs. Perkins introduced Clock Partners in her class, she allowed students to choose all four of their appointments, with plans to change them up every month or so. This helped ensure that learners had an opportunity to collaborate with a variety of others throughout the year. At the start of the lesson, Mrs. Perkins introduced the learning target and success criteria, and students partnered up with their 3 o'clock partner to reflect on the learning goals around the learning QAR.

Mrs. Perkins found that students quickly decided on a spot in the room to host a standing conversation with their 3 o'clock partners. They discussed the learning target and predicted what they would do to achieve the success criteria. As students talked, Mrs. Perkins positioned herself close to students she was specifically interested in hearing how they were thinking about the goal. After she heard several teams interpreting the purpose of the lesson accurately, she chose not to share the purpose with the whole group. There was no reason to repeat multiple conversations and expend valuable instructional time. She affirmed they were ready to get down to learning, sent them back to their seats, and moved on to the next phase of the lesson.

Because she needed to establish basic knowledge, Mrs. Perkins provided a visual and offered a brief instruction approach to four concepts from the lesson. One by one, as she shared each definition, she embedded opportunities for students to use Choral Response, offering repetition that reinforced the new vocabulary. Mrs. Perkins knew that once her students had the definitions down, they would be ready to apply their knowledge.

When Mrs. Perkins had enough evidence to show her that most students understood the four concepts, she sent them off with a different Clock Partner to define the concepts in their own words.

Once again, I watched her seek out specific students and listen to their definitions. It was obvious that she had chosen those students intentionally.

This process was more efficient and more effective than calling on a single hand in the air. If she had wanted to hear from a specific student and used the raise-your-hand routine, she would have had to single that student out in front of the entire class with the traditional method. Instead, her approach provided every student an opportunity to talk, and allowed her to check in on the students she wanted to monitor.

In the next part of the lesson, students had to apply their definitions. Mrs. Perkins provided a question related to the text and students had to identify what type of question it was. She first tried Choral Response with the whole group again, but now that students were moving to a higher-level skill of analyzing a question and applying a new definition, there was a bit more struggle. Choral Responses showed that not all the students were able to identify the question type. Because the response was quick and simultaneous, Mrs. Perkins could not identify who knew and who did not. So she switched to another action that still assumed all hands were up and would provide her with a better picture of who was struggling. She used a Standing Poll.

Students were assigned to small groups and given a piece of text with sample questions. Within their groups, they had to determine what type of questions they had. When they were finished in their small groups, she asked them to compare their conclusions with others. They used handheld whiteboards called KleenSlates to write their responses, and though they worked in groups, each student was still accountable for writing on a KleenSlate. On the count of three, they revealed their answers to one another, rather than just to her. They could then compare their responses to those of other groups and ask questions to find out why some groups had different ideas. This was a common procedure in her class, and all the students knew to begin inquiring about other groups' thinking.

The lesson provided all students with multiple opportunities to respond, held everyone accountable, and gave Mrs. Perkins an indication that students were successful. She knew the students had support from peers in their small groups. So, in order to measure individual learning, the lesson closed with a four-question, low-stakes quiz to be sure they met the learning target, tying it back to the success criteria.

Hand raising has been a tradition for a long time in schools. Early in their academic careers, students are taught that if they want to speak, they should raise their hands and wait their turns. But it is an ineffective design for achieving success for all students. When our approach to teaching and learning embraces all phases of the learning process, we must move beyond the ping-pong approach of Q&A and actually check for understanding. Instead of accepting a few responses as representative of the entire class, replace the one-question-one-student approach to engagement with opportunities for all students to process a lesson. Hold *everyone* accountable for actively learning.

Using strategies that engage everyone in your questions will help you reveal a truer picture of whether students are learning and what you need to do if they are not. If we are going to make assumptions about students' eagerness to learn, why not assume that they all have their hands raised, and are pumped, primed, and waiting for the opportunity?

The argument against calling on one hand at a time is that we are inviting students to disengage by doing nothing. Don't raise your hand and you won't be called on. Don't raise your hand and you won't have to take a risk. Don't raise your hand and it is acceptable to not think or learn.

No teacher plans to send these messages. But we do every day when we say, "Raise your hand if you can tell me ..."

HACK 2

KICK THE IDK BUCKET
KEEP THE COGNITIVE BATON
IN STUDENTS' HANDS

*You're in charge of your mind. You can help
it grow by using it the right way.*
— CAROL DWECK, MINDSET AUTHOR AND RESEARCHER

THE PROBLEM: STUDENTS USE "I DON'T KNOW" RESPONSES AS A WAY OUT

WHEN TEACHERS ARE delivering content or thinking of questions, they bear much of the cognitive load. The plan, of course, is to pass the baton over to students and have them hold on to it for as long as possible. When a student gives an IDK response, though, they essentially are refusing to accept the baton. Shrugged shoulders, blank stares, and unproductive conversation fillers such as "uhhh" are all categorized the same. They are all labeled as IDK responses. In each case, the student is avoiding cognitive or social engagement.

Of course, at times kids offer IDK as knee-jerk reactions. Maybe because they don't immediately know an answer, or because they have had success deflecting academic attention by giving a confused look that suggests they might not know.

No matter the reason, IDK answers are a problem in the classroom. Accepting them as responses only magnifies the problem. Students learn that if they wish to avoid effort or risk, the ticket is "I don't know." Sometimes these words are stated explicitly. Other times, they offer dead silence, leaving the teacher wondering what to do next. Wait it out? Move on to someone else? Offer a hint?

What makes this problem even more complex is that we are often unsure of *why* students are unwilling to take a risk and engage in thought. Some are so automatic in their responses that we wonder if they really do not know how to respond, or are just shy, or are actively disengaged.

Matching our reaction to the reasoning behind a student's IDK allows us to react appropriately—and control who is holding that cognitive baton.

THE HACK: KICK THE IDK BUCKET

We set ourselves up to kick the IDK bucket by identifying the root cause for the "I don't know" response. You see, we cannot assume that IDK means the student really does not know something. Sure, that's a potential trigger, but it isn't the only one. Each reason has a different solution.

The careful pairing of problems with counteractions will send the IDK bucket to the graveyard.

Picture a cognitive baton. Your key to reducing the number of IDKs in your classroom is to keep the cognitive baton in the student's possession. The person holding the cognitive baton is the person doing the most mental work. Why are the students trying to rid themselves of the cognitive baton? One reason is that many students have come to believe that the game of school is about knowing answers. The narrative on this must change. Students do not have to know the answers. They just cannot be satisfied with *not* knowing them.

In short, IDK should be a rise to action, not an end result. We need to see this as a starting point, rather than a final answer. There are bound to be underlying reasons why they are unwilling to take a chance. "I don't know" is safe from the risk of being wrong. It does not require vulnerability. It does not draw the spotlight.

When students can identify the root cause of their IDK, and find a way around it, they are one step closer to removing the barriers that are delaying their understanding.

No easy, one-size-fits-all answer exists here. Facing an IDK situation does not trigger one specific formulaic procedure for overcoming it. We have to consider *multiple* reasons why a student might be avoiding answering or giving a wrong answer. Use Image 2.1 to help identify the root cause. When students can identify the root cause of their IDK, and find a way around it, they are one step closer to removing the barriers that are delaying their understanding.

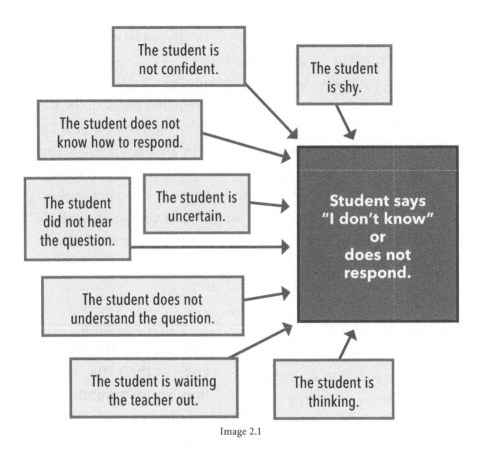

Image 2.1

Creating a classroom where students feel safe about taking risks doesn't happen without purposeful efforts by the teacher to create the culture. How we respond to students when they don't know an answer says a lot about whether we value learning ... or just the right answer. Accessing the student's reasoning for the IDK helps the teacher determine whether the student lacks confidence, was disengaged, has a misconception, or is really lost on a particular concept. Use the table in Image 2.2 to align your strategy to kick the IDK bucket with the reason for the IDK. This will decrease how often you hear students using those words as their final answers.

Reason for IDK	Strategy	Comments
Student did not hear the question	Repeat the question	Restate the question exactly the same way as it was asked the first time. Many times, teachers begin to give too many hints when repeating questions, therefore lowering the cognitive demand for students.
Student did not understand the question	Rephrase the question at the same level, or ask if there's a word they need to have defined	Q: What strategy did you uses to solve the problem? 1. Do you know what I mean when I ask for a "strategy"? 2. How did you solve the problem?
Student is thinking	WAIT	• Wait time is often the best prompt. You might confirm the student needs wait time by asking "Do you need some time to think?" • Provide wait time for everyone before you even call on a student. That way the attention on one student isn't so uncomfortable
Student is bashful	Use a student talk protocol like turn and ask	Listen in on the conversation of a shy student. Ask his permission to call on him to share, and then stay close to him as he gives his response to the class. Proximity can be reassuring for shy students.
Student is not confident	Allow the student to quantify a response	Use the power of "might." Adding it to a question softens it significantly. What is the solution? What might be a solution?
Student is accustomed to getting more clues, so she is waiting the teacher out	Break the pattern of over-prompting	Be prepared with several responses if you think the students are waiting you out. Remember that if you're uncomfortable with the silence, they probably are too. WAIT.
These strategies apply to individual, small group, large group, and whole class instruction.		

Image 2.2

WHAT YOU CAN DO TOMORROW

Eradicating "I don't know" from your classroom will take un-training. Try these strategies and notice how students begin to accept responsibility for learning instead of taking the easy way out by saying IDK.

- **Use a physical object as your cognitive baton.** Use a ball, stuffed animal, or actual baton to designate a speaker. I use an actual cognitive baton or a think stick. Having students hold an object when they have the floor provides a visual and kinesthetic reminder that it is their turn to contribute their thoughts. That symbolic cognitive baton signals to them that they have the floor and you are willing to wait for their reply. If they attempt to slip in an IDK, the cognitive baton will be physically passed to you—at which point you know not to accept it. Instead, use a bucket-kicking strategy.

- **Be ready with encouraging responses that keep the baton in their hands.** If a student gives an IDK, use these prompts to help organize the student's thinking. Do not dummy down a question or begin to answer it for the student. Keep these IDK bucket-kicker questions prepped and ready:

- What would you say if you did know?
- What can you rule out?
- What are you thinking so far?
- Think aloud. Let us hear what your brain is processing.
- Tell us what parts you're sure of and what parts you're still working through.
- What part has you stuck?

- **Invite students to qualify their thoughts.** You can hear a lack of confidence in a student's words. In these cases, students use IDK to avoid committing to an answer they aren't sure about. When you suspect a student is reticent to reply, instead of affirming or redirecting the answers, encourage qualifiers like:

  - Right now, I'm thinking …
  - Based on the little bit I know currently …
  - I might change my mind later, but here's where I am now …
  - I'm still thinking this through …
  - I'm not exactly sure, so let me take a shot at it …

These all send the message that students do not have to be 100-percent certain. They offer an under-commitment to their answers.

- **Seek qualifiers instead of commitments.** Perfectionists live within our classroom walls. These students have the most trouble committing to their answers because they are still wrestling with the notion that it is acceptable not to know. These students can be 95-percent confident in their thinking and still offer an IDK in place of taking a risk. An answer for these students is to create a mathematical win-win. Ask them to estimate the likelihood that their response is correct. Encourage them to share their thinking, and leave the door open for it to be wrong by quantifying it.

  It is socially acceptable to quantify our answers. How many times have you used, "I'm 99.9-percent positive" or "I'm only 30-percent sure"? If a student is only 40-percent sure the answer is correct, it means the student is 60-percent sure it's not. When it turns out their solution was off-base, it means they were right that they were wrong. Now you have a perfect opportunity to stress the importance of recognizing where there might be holes in your thinking. We have to get the message across to students that it is okay—even normal—not to be sure about something. Take away the reason for the IDK response if a student isn't sure about an answer.

- **Allow questions as responses.** Rather than demanding an answer, invite students to share questions they have about a question. This gives them a chance to gain clarity and deepen knowledge through effective questioning. Encourage students to explore their natural curiosity. Allow them to verbalize an inquiry related to the topic and begin a dialogue. This also offers an acceptable alternative to silence and blank stares.

- **Acknowledge students for their effort, not their answers.** Praising learners for correct answers can discourage students from taking risks. Many students use this praise to define themselves. They personalize correct/incorrect answers in a way that supports a fixed mindset that they either are smart or not smart. Accolades for a correct answer are temporary, and can be replaced with a negative self-image when the next answer is incorrect. Applauding positive learning behaviors is consistent regardless of whether the student knows the right answer or is still figuring it out. Effort, persistence, creative thinking, problem-solving, and reflection are all traits that will serve students long past knowing the answer to question number four. Search for ways to highlight good thinking, not just good answers. See examples of this in Image 2.3. This practice will build stamina for when students are faced with difficult or challenging situations.

Frame Feedback Around Thinking	
Don't Focus on Student or Answer	**Focus on Thinking**
Yes, that's right.	You were reading carefully.
You are so smart.	You are really giving your brain a workout today.
I know this is hard for you. Just do your best.	I know this is challenging. With effort, you will keep improving.
Great answer.	All that work paid off. Good thing you didn't give up.
No. That's not right.	What can we learn from this?
That's not quite what I was looking for.	I can follow your thinking. I see how you came to that conclusion.
See? It's easy. Right?	Your thinking seems to be working. Looks like you're understanding it now.

Image 2.3

A BLUEPRINT FOR FULL IMPLEMENTATION

Step 1: Communicate to students that it is okay not to know, and follow it with a plan for how they can gain the knowledge.

Creating a learning space where it is acceptable to be wrong is only half the solution. It is an important skill to be able to self-assess what you know or do not know. Knowing that will help students know what to do about it. It is like having the check engine light come on in your car. If you do not know how to assess and fix the problem, most people will not merely shrug their shoulders and keep driving as if nothing is wrong. If we do not know the answer ourselves, we develop a plan to get an answer. We might ask a friend, look in the manual, research possibilities online, or even take the car to a mechanic. The point is that just knowing there is a problem is not a solution in itself. We need to take the next step to solve it.

When we accept IDK responses, do nothing to fill those gaps, then wonder why students perform poorly on any type of assessment, it is like continuing to drive with your check engine light on, then scratching your head when the engine seizes and you're stuck on the side of the road.

Step 2: Create an IDK anchor chart.

It will be frustrating for students if we talk out of both sides of our mouths by saying it is okay not to know, and at the same time, telling them they are not allowed to say, "I don't know." Instead, we can give them solutions. Part of being responsible learners is knowing how to take action to help themselves.

A visual list of acceptable responses empowers students to take control of their own learning while giving you a glimpse of where the problem lies. Develop this list with your students, starting with potential substitutions for the common IDK response, like:

- Please repeat the question.
- I need to think about that for a minute, please.
- I'm not sure I understand the question, could you rephrase it, please?
- What does the word _____ mean?
- Could I hear the question in my native language?
- May I have more information about _____, please?
- I would like to ask a clarifying question.
- Let me check some resources to help me.

Step 3: Do not allow students to pass the cognitive baton.

One option that often pops up when brainstorming non-IDK responses is "phone a friend," which comes from the game show *Who Wants to Be a Millionaire*. When contestants on the show are unsure of an answer, they are given three options, or lifelines.

1. Ask the audience, where the audience is polled on how they would answer the question.

2. 50:50, where two of the four possible answers are removed, cutting the choices in half.

3. Phone a friend, where the contestant calls someone on their list and asks what the person would say.

This third lifeline is popular in classrooms. Not every teacher calls it phone a friend. Some say, "Would you like to ask someone for help?" Or worse, the teacher simply gets tired of waiting and invites the class to intervene by asking, "Who can help?" This is an alteration from the original lifeline. In the show, the host asks a question and the contestant is responsible for answering it. Sure, the contestant can seek the perspective of a friend, but ultimately, the contestant is still responsible for making meaning out of what that friend said. The contestant holds the cognitive baton the entire time.

In classrooms, phone a friend begins similarly. The host asks the contestant, in this case the student, a question. When the student does not know the answer, they are invited to get help from someone in the classroom. So far, the analogy aligns. What happens next in the classroom is where the key difference emerges. On the game show, the contestant speaks to the friend while the audience and the host listen to their conversation. They talk to each other and try to make meaning together. In a classroom, this looks more like the host retracting the question from the contestant and offering it to the friend. It allows the original student to pass the cognitive load to someone else, making that person the replacement player. This is not helpful to the wannabe millionaire.

In the newest version of *Who Wants to Be a Millionaire*, the third lifeline has been updated. Instead of phone a friend, it is now called "plus one." There is no longer a phone call, but the contestant invites a predetermined person to join them on stage. Together, they talk through the question. The friend offers an idea for the contestant to consider before the contestant gives the final answer. This structure keeps the ownership on the same person, yet allows for support if needed.

If you choose to include phone a friend on your list of allowable IDK responses, be sure to clarify that phone a friend does not mean pass the baton. It means plus one. That way, you give the student a path forward in learning, rather than allowing them to escape responding at all.

Step 4: Host an IDK funeral.

As a ceremonial end to answering with "I don't know" in your classroom, host an IDK funeral. You want students to look at IDK through two lenses. First, highlight the fact that there are many things they, and you, currently don't know. On one color of paper, ask them to write anything they do not know yet. These can be things they wish they knew, or far-reaching skills/experiences like not knowing how to pilot a spaceship. The purpose of this first round is to recognize that it's okay not to know something.

Next, point them to thinking about why they give IDK answers. On a different color paper, ask them to explore some of the root causes for saying they don't know. Reveal that you are aware that students use IDK when they might actually know, or at least have an idea. Guide them to reflect on what other influences might cause IDK answers.

Accept all their responses without comment. This is not the time to "Yeah, but ..." how they feel. If a student says he says IDK because he doesn't think his ideas are good enough, write it down without discussion. Do not pause to debate their root causes, just collect them all in a big pile of IDK whys.

Now it's time for the service. Be as elaborate or casual as you like. You can ask students to write a eulogy for their IDK or offer final goodbyes yourself. Determine whether the final resting spot for IDK answers will be a burial or cremation. Then get rid of them. Dig a hole behind the school and throw their IDKs and IDK whys in the dirt, or for a more dramatic end to IDK's life, burn the paper.

(Please check fire regulations and get permission before sparking your IDK campfire, to prevent your funeral from violating school safety guidelines.)

Step 5: Label the actions students took.

Now that you have removed the IDKs from your classroom, revisit episodes when students used something other than IDK. Calling these to attention can reinforce the behaviors that ultimately lead to success and learning. For example, you might narrate the following event: "I noticed that when you didn't understand the question, you were very specific in asking what *reciprocate* means. Once you got clarity on the question, you were able to offer your detailed thoughts. I see your IDK isn't rising from the ashes."

This type of labeling elevates student status with public recognition, reinforces norms for learning, and highlights that the knowledge was there all along; it was interpreting the question that created the student's hesitation.

OVERCOMING PUSHBACK

Being put on the spot can create anxiety for students. A reasonable amount of discomfort is acceptable. Learning is hard, so we can expect that initially, students might become uneasy if they're not allowed their IDK answers. The idea behind having students hold on to the cognitive baton does not have to come with a spotlight shining upon them. One simple distraction that does not let the student off the hook is a quick Turn and Talk. Prompt the other students to discuss the question with their shoulder partner. This will allow time for you to walk over to the student and reassure them, in order to reduce anxiety.

It is easier to just tell them. Easier? Probably for the teacher. Less effective? Certainly. Learning is not easy work, and taking the path of least resistance should not be the default. If your best strategy when you are faced with an IDK final answer is to tell students what to think, you are in for a long and painful year of fatigue and frustration. It is the cognitive struggle that solidifies understanding for learners. Simply telling them over and over is maddening—and will only reinforce the IDK. They have to process key points to the lesson, and listening—active or not—is not the best way to trigger neurons. And "no new neurons" prevents new learning, which will retrigger IDK responses.

Some students say IDK so they don't have to participate. Sounds like you have already identified the root cause. If the reason they give an IDK response is that they are trying to blend in, incorporate movement. Students who use IDK as a way to avoid participation do not want to stand out. If everyone else is out of their seats, the student who is not participating and remains sitting still in the seat is garnering attention. In order to fulfill their preference to blend in, they must stand up and participate in the class movement. Use the exercises we've talked about (and those in the Appendix) to change the environment and encourage the students who don't want to participate to look at things in a different way.

THE HACK IN ACTION

Teachers often use job charts to develop responsibility, a sense of community, and to foster leadership skills. One third-grade teacher, Mrs. Maureen Jorgensen, has a unique title on her chart: Class Brain.

Initially, the student assigned as the Class Brain had the duty of standing next to her when she was providing a Think Aloud during reading instruction. The Brain was the personified idea that she was speaking her thoughts aloud as she had them. Even as an expert reader, when faced with a complex text, Mrs. Jorgensen still had to think. (Find tips to leverage Think Alouds in Hack 6: Fill Your Back Pocket.) As she read aloud, Mrs. Jorgensen would choose a particularly challenging spot in the text, and stop. With a perplexed look, she would say, "Brain?" Then the Class Brain would stand beside her as she verbally processed how she was addressing her IDK moment.

One day, when I was visiting Mrs. Jorgensen's class during math, she asked a student to answer a question. He gave an answer, and because Mrs. Jorgensen had trained herself to listen for "right thinking" (see Hack 8: Hear the Music, for more on this), she followed up by asking him to explain how he got that answer. No response. He stared at her as she provided appropriate think time, and even glanced at her "Instead of IDK" anchor chart, but it didn't work. Finally, he blurted out the words we try so desperately to avoid. "I … don't … know."

She gave him a half-smile and reminded him that it is okay not to know, but it is not okay not to try. So she asked him what he needed to help himself.

This young man shyly suggested, "I think I need the Brain."

Before this moment, Mrs. Jorgensen had not considered students using the Brain to think aloud, but she did what any teacher should do: She rolled with it. She signaled the Class Brain to stand over his peer's head and hold up a visual image of a brain. It was magical, like how a kiss on a toddler's boo-boo makes the pain go away. That reluctant mathematician began justifying his response using math vocabulary simply because he was triggered to access his brain.

Now, Mrs. Jorgensen can ask to hear students' brains. This is a well-developed norm in the classroom and she uses it to problem-solve, justify, clarify, or whatever students need to help them persevere in their thinking. Imagine that: Tell kids to use their brains, and they do!

Using "I don't know" is a learned behavior that students have mastered through years of classroom interactions. They often are successful in avoiding struggle when content doesn't come easily, because giving an IDK response will either prompt the teacher to call on someone else or make the question easier. When we focus on thinking beyond the IDK reply and celebrate engagement and effort, the students are less likely to be self-conscious about not knowing the right answers. Instead, they start to realize that learning is messy and often takes work and time.

We dummy down learning opportunities when we assume that an "I don't know" or student silence requires cues, reteaching, or lowering the level of questioning. Before jumping to a remediation, verify whether there is another reason for a lack of response, give students ways to articulate what is interfering with their ability to answer a question, support a growth mindset culture by encouraging them to take risks, and hold them accountable for engaging in the learning. Using these Hacks will reduce the number of times you hear "I don't know" as a first response from students.

Responding to IDK responses is not a science. Certain situations can be sensitive and the teacher should handle them individually, because relationships will always outlast a single lesson. They are also difficult to repair when damaged. So honor the student's dignity while maintaining an expectation that we are here to learn. Every one of us.

HACK 3

PUNCTUATE YOUR LEARNING TIME
CLOSE WITH REFLECTION QUESTIONS

*We do not learn from experience... we
learn from reflecting on experience.*
— John Dewey, Philosopher and Educational Reformer

THE PROBLEM: LEARNING TIME
DOESN'T INCLUDE CLOSURE

TIME IS ONE of our most valuable commodities in education. It is also one of the most challenging areas to manage. We have so many variables when trying to account for time within a lesson, and even the most carefully planned lessons rarely align perfectly with the allocated minutes for each part.

Most teachers have learned to be flexible with time by developing backup plans. We tell ourselves, "If there is enough time, I'll add this" and "If I am running short on time, I'll skip that." Closing a lesson is rarely on the list of lesson components designated to skip. But it happens way too often.

When we don't button up a task with intentional closure, we increase the likelihood that students will walk away without linking their actions to their learning. Teachers regularly attempt to address this lack of connection by starting the next day's lesson with a refresher. "Let's think about what we did yesterday." But there are two problems with this process:

1. The statement focuses on doing and not learning.

2. The opportunity to capitalize on students making meaning immediately, then building on that meaning the next day, is lost.

When a lesson begins with processing yesterday's learning, it's no longer an activation of prior knowledge. Now it's a reflection that requires students to recall details that they have probably forgotten.

It might seem like an efficient use of time or a logical decision to combine closing the previous day's lesson with today's opening. When you dig into the benefits of a closure and the reasons for an opening, however, they have different purposes. Wrapping up a lesson by deliberately focusing students' attention on what they learned is an acutely different type of thinking than triggering a memory. Lesson closure helps students frame the memory so they can use it in the future. It is best to activate this reflection when it is fresh in your students' minds.

Cognitively shifting students' attention to what they have learned as a result of engaging in the lesson is a critical part of every lesson. I would go so far as to say it is not negotiable. This is true even when the lesson runs long, and the task is continued into the next day. Relate it to your own daily routine. Don't you feel frazzled when you have to leave school quickly and do not have time to process the day and think about tomorrow? We naturally build in closure to our day—even if we did not finish what we set out to accomplish. Some of us even talk to ourselves. "Students struggled with XYZ, so tomorrow I will need to address that concept. I do not want to simply tell them, so I need to figure out a way to help them realize their own misconceptions."

This simplistic look back on what happened today, what that means, and how it impacts tomorrow is a reflection. If you didn't take a moment to consciously close up the day and organize it mentally, you will feel unprepared for the next one. Activating prior knowledge is not the same as processing. Each holds a critical role in the learning process.

THE HACK: PUNCTUATE YOUR LEARNING TIME

To punctuate your learning time is to bring it to a purposeful and intentional closure. Notice this Hack is punctuating your *learning time*. Planning a closure for the end of a lesson plan might not be the same as coming to the end of a specific learning block. Some lessons are intended to start and finish in a single slotted time, and this is the easiest punctuation to see. We close these lessons with a period. Sometimes an exclamation point! They are short and sweet and seamlessly closed at the end of a time block. Other lessons, though, wrap up midway through the block of minutes, or extend beyond the class time. These are the lessons most at risk

EXIT TICKETS

Check for Understanding	Relevance	Self Assessment	Mindset
• 3-2-1: 3 - things you learned 2 - ways you supported your own learning 1 - question you still have	• How will today's learning help you as a reader (author, mathematician, scientist, artist, musician, etc.)?	• Tomorrow's Help Scale: 4 - I can help someone else 3 - I will not need any help 2 - I might need help from my resources 1 - I will need help from an expert	• What kind of self talk did you have? Was it encouraging, negative, helpful, etc.?
• What did you learn as a result of today's lesson?	• When might this learning be helpful to you outside of the classroom?	• How Sure Are You? Respond to a check for understanding question. Then quantify your level of confidence in your response with a percent.	• How did you approach something that was difficult for you today?
• 6 Word Summary: In exactly six words, sum up the big idea of today's learning.	• Why is it important that you learn about _____ (insert learning target)?		• How did your mindset impact your learning today?
• Ask a broken record question. (See Hack 5)	• What kind of careers use this type of learning?	• What do you need to learn next?	• What level of effort was required for your learning today?
			• How were you challenged today? What pushed your thinking?

Image 3.1

of getting shortchanged of their proper attention. In these cases, you should end the lesson with a comma or a question mark. They should never stop abruptly, or without a natural conclusion.

When the class period nears its end at the same time as the lesson is finishing, we have a natural time for reflection. Many teachers use a variety of structures that pose formative questions to students, and are developed to assess whether students met the learning target. These can also determine whether students see the relevance in their learning. Another option is to give students the opportunity to self-assess their learning and identify any remaining gaps. Regardless, they should pull the lesson together, assess the learning, and help to set it in the students' minds.

A common structure for this is the exit ticket. See Image 3.1 for ways that exit tickets can be designed for different reflection purposes.

If teachers take a few minutes to reflect on the productivity of today and establish a plan for tomorrow, it will undoubtedly make tomorrow more efficient.

Regardless of the specific purpose, in all cases, students are reflecting on their learning. They are punctuating their learning time with metacognitive thoughts. After thinking about content, we want students to think about their thinking by summarizing it and tucking it away in their brains for future retrieval.

On days when the lesson is designed to continue into the next day, or unexpectedly runs long, you might think about waiting until the lesson is over to offer a reflection. But the purpose of closure is to summarize a chunk of time. Doing so—even in the middle of a lesson—allows you to more seamlessly pick up the learning where it left off. On days when learning does not fit perfectly into your given timeframe, it is even more important to activate metacognition, because you know you're going to continue the lesson later. Consider the following scenarios when lessons took longer than the teacher had hoped:

No punctuation

Day 1: "Oops, looks like we are out of time. We will pick up tomorrow where we left off."

Day 2: "Let's remember where we left off yesterday. What do we need to finish up today? How much time do you think you need?"

Punctuation

Day 1: "Oops, looks like we are going to run out of time. Let's pause for today and reflect on what we learned, then set a plan for tomorrow. How much time should we reserve to execute that plan?"

Day 2: "Yesterday we didn't have quite enough time to meet all of our goals. Turn and ask your partner what they need to accomplish today. We reserved ten minutes for this. I'll start the timer."

The punctuated lesson models responsibility, time management, and goal-setting, and brings students into their learning plan. The day after a punctuated lesson, students come to the lesson prepared. The teacher activates the students to put their plan into motion and, as an added benefit, also has an idea of how much time to allocate for students to fulfill their learning plans. In the unpunctuated example, the teacher has unintentionally modeled the process of building the plane while it's being flown. If teachers take a few minutes to reflect on the productivity of today and establish a plan for tomorrow, it will undoubtedly make tomorrow more efficient.

In classrooms with younger students, this reflection process might be better conducted as a whole group. Record the class's plan on chart paper and pull it out the following day as a reminder of the goals you and your students developed, and to get ready for a productive day.

You might be surprised at how much students have learned even without completing a task. I recall a high school English Language Arts (ELA) teacher who was leading a lesson on character development. She was using the opportunity to practice couplets from a previous unit, and in the lesson, gave students trinkets she had collected. They included things like novelty keychains, glitter nail polish, and a postage stamp. She asked groups of students to use the items to develop a character and then write a poem with thirteen couplets to describe that character.

As time ticked by, she worried that students were not going to have time to complete their entire poems. She thought she was going to have to reserve time the next day for them to finish. She chose to pause their writing and ask them to individually explain how they'd used the random items to develop a complex character.

After class, when we met to reflect on the lesson, the teacher shared her elation with the quality and depth of characters the students created. Every group met or exceeded her expectations, even though none of them had finished all thirteen couplets. She was able to use the data she received in the lesson closure to forego finishing the poems. There was no need. Students had met the target and provided evidence of their learning without completing the task. Instead of practicing more couplets, she was ready to add to their character development and move into the next lesson.

WHAT YOU CAN DO TOMORROW

The most challenging part of punctuating your lesson is to reserve time for closure. The following ideas will support your effort to structure your lesson in a way that, even if closure comes in the final minutes of a lesson, it is not at the bottom of the priority list.

- **Bring it back to the learning target.** A fail-proof closure for any lesson is to bring the learning target back into the limelight. Ask students to comment on their progress toward meeting the target. Options include:
  - What part of our learning target are you most confident in today?
  - Where do you still need more practice or thinking to have met today's learning target?
  - How much support did you need to meet today's learning target?
  - Would you classify this learning target as comfortable or challenging? Why?

  Their responses can be written on scraps of paper, left on sticky notes for you to review, documented in learning journals, shared with

shoulder partners, communicated verbally on the way out the door, or in any other quick way that raises accountability. Many teachers have gone to thumbs-up if you got it, thumbs-sideways if you are getting it, or thumbs-down if you aren't there yet. I admit, this is better than no closure at all, but not by much. Students tend to provide a thumbs-up without much reflection, and it doesn't give room for discussion or true measurement. Scanning a room of thirty thumbs in a second or two is a challenge for even the best set of teacher eyes.

Collecting something tangible or creating a dialogue about learning will improve the quality of thought that students dedicate to truly reflecting on their progress toward meeting the learning target. Opt for concrete documentation if you have plans to use their reflections in small-group instruction, interventions, or differentiation of any kind. Relying on memory hours later to plan these follow-up supports often leads to biased placement of students.

- **Clean up before you wrap up.** If we really want a summary of the learning to be the last thing on students' minds, it has to be the last agenda item. For that reason, it might be convenient to wrap up a lesson at the end of student work time. You can punctuate the closure more powerfully if students clean up and reflect on the lesson after they have put their materials away. When students are putting their materials away while the teacher is summarizing the learning for the class period, their cognitive attention is weak at best. Students have already shut down and are shifting their focus to the next task or leaving the room. Designating time to tidy up and center their thinking on lesson reflection honors its value. If you would not begin a lesson until students were ready to engage, why would you close a lesson without their full concentration?

- **Use a timer.** Nothing's wrong with modeling how to use tools to meet goals, and this can help you kill two birds with one stone. Time is a factor that students often struggle to manage. Set a visible timer for a learning task, leaving enough time to activate a proper closure. This will not only assist you in protecting time to punctuate your lesson, but will also give students a sense of how they are progressing toward a task or goal. Making time visible to everyone invites you and your students to monitor the precious minutes you have together. Even if the students have not completed their task, the timer will serve as a reminder that class is about to end, and that it is time to transition to reflection on what was learned—or not learned—during the lesson.

- **Warm up and cool down.** When exercising, you begin a workout with a warmup. You stretch muscles and slowly increase your heart rate to improve blood flow. The warmup is important so you can perform well and avoid injury. Likewise, at the end of a fitness activity, you gradually slow down to allow your pulse to return to normal and cool your body down before jumping in your car to head home. Your lessons with students deserve this same attention. Think of your lesson closure as your cool down to learning. Your purpose is to let the knowledge settle in, and help students file the information for easy retrieval in future lessons or use in their everyday lives.

A BLUEPRINT FOR FULL IMPLEMENTATION

Step 1: Build an agenda for your lesson plan and do the math.

Though it is difficult to predict exactly how long each portion of your lesson will take, an estimation is better than a wait-and-see approach. How you begin your lesson sets the tone. How you end it helps determine what students take away from it. Consider the components of a lesson, and be sure to include time to move from one task to the next. Plan for chunks of time to distribute materials, allow students to travel through the classroom, and other similar transitions.

Take the extra step to tally up those minutes. You can avoid being surprised that you are short on time if you find that you estimated your fifty-minute block to hold a seventy-five-minute lesson. If your best prediction totals forty-five minutes before the closure, you can be mindful to include brevity as a criterion for planning the very end of your lesson.

Step 2: Create reflection journals.

Having a place to record reflections allows you to take better advantage of those reflections. Keeping them in a spiral notebook or folder allows students to see the progression of their learning. This is valuable on two levels.

First, students who are writing in reflection journals have the opportunity to make connections in content in one tidy place. As their knowledge builds over time, they can monitor how they got from point A to point B. Educators help students connect the parts to the whole. The big-picture approach balances details with big ideas. Hammering the pieces of learning can give both teachers and students a false assumption that students have a deep insight into a concept just because they have many surface-level understandings. A reflection journal will show how deeply they're taking those points of daily learning.

It's even more powerful to use reflection journals to prompt students to comment on their mindsets. Ask them to document their struggle and perseverance so they can think about them later. Encourage them to write about the days when learning was a challenge, followed by the strategies they used to overcome those challenges.

Journals encourage reflection on both self and the learning, and make valuable endpoints to lessons—as well as places to start, if you've interrupted a lesson.

Step 3: Work backward.

To protect the sacred time for reflection, try planning in reverse. Start with your closure in mind. Designate a minimum number of minutes for your conclusion, and mark the clock time. For example, if class ends at 9:50 and you want a minimum of eight minutes for the closure, mark 9:42 as the last possible minute to move into the punctuation. Knowing when you've scheduled the punctuation to begin will help you make on-the-spot decisions about whether or not to take advantage of a teachable moment, choose to have students share with their peers, or include other time suckers that steal from your closure.

I have heard countless teachers look back on how time was allocated in the lesson and wish they had shortened something other than the wrap-up. Since the closure is not negotiable, something else has to be. Find wiggle room in your lesson. The closer your wiggle room is to the end of the lesson, the more likely you are to preserve your time for reflection.

Step 4: Advertise your punctuation.

In addition to punctuating your learning time, advertise it. Sharing the daily agenda gives students the big picture of how the flow of learning will transpire. Add closure on your agenda. A posted visual that includes the closing event will be a reminder throughout the lesson. You know that if you miss it, you will have at least one darling who will happily remind you that you forgot the closure.

Step 5: Mark it.

Close with a simple question: What punctuation fits best with our learning today? Not a bad way to spiral in a little grammar, either. See Image 3.2 for examples of how students can punctuate their learning.

PUNCTUATE YOUR LEARNING		
,	Apostrophe	Something is missing. I know what I still need to learn.
,	Comma	I understand parts of today's learning. I still have more to learn.
...	Ellipsis	I'm still in the process of learning. I need more time or practice.
!	Exclamation Point	I am excited about this learning. I understand and am ready for the next challenge!
?	Question Mark	I still have questions. I am feeling confused.
" "	Quotation Marks	I can explain this to someone else.
.	Period	I understand what I was supposed to learn today. I was able to successfully complete learning tasks.
;	Semicolon	I see how to connect this learning to something else that is relevant.

Image 3.2

OVERCOMING PUSHBACK

Barriers to making lesson closure a priority are more logistical than they are philosophical. Time is a resource that educators are constantly managing. Everything we do requires time, and it all seems important. Finding shortcuts is often a survival tactic. But we should never let it stop us from achieving our mission.

There is never enough time. True. And because this is true, it is crucial that we use the limited time to maximize learning. Five more minutes of engaging in a task are not as likely to impact students as five minutes of reflection. In the long run, it will cost you more time if you must recap it for them the next day.

When students are actively engaged, I do not want to stop them from being productive just to close the lesson. It is joyous to see students who are excited about learning. When they are engrossed in a learning activity, it is hard to stop them. Bring purpose to what students are doing by connecting it to what they are learning. Doing so keeps the perspective on the big picture of making school meaningful. Think of it as taking time to smell the roses. Allow yourself to reap the full benefits of a well-executed lesson by highlighting how students increased their knowledge. You fall short of the full impact when you don't ignite the *aha* spark.

I can start tomorrow with a summary of today's lesson. You're robbing Peter to pay Paul. Pushing a closure to tomorrow's introduction only displaces an intentional lesson launch. The effectiveness of *two* lessons is now potentially diminished. Today's lesson is compromised because it wasn't tied back together. Students might have left the learning time with different takeaways, or worse, no connection to learning at all. Tomorrow's lesson is not its best because the introduction doesn't serve a single purpose. A conclusion is not the same as an introduction. Avoid using them interchangeably just for your convenience. Just ask a writing teacher.

THE HACK IN ACTION

One of my favorite rooms to visit was an ELA class led by Mrs. Barb Aguirre. When planning lessons for her sixth-grade students, she was crystal clear on what she wanted them to learn. Mrs. Aguirre's experience told her that students often struggled with the shift from opinion writing to argumentative writing, so she created a lesson about that—and shared her end goal with her students:

> *Develop an argument paragraph for why all schools in MI should or should not go to a year-round calendar. Begin by making a clear, debatable claim. Provide at least three pieces of evidence to support and prove your claim, including one piece of evidence from a credible secondary source. End your paragraph with a strong statement that summarizes your point.*

Mrs. Aguirre identified learning progressions her students needed to have before being able to tackle this argumentative piece of writing. To establish a purpose for each day's lesson, she chose to provide the big picture for students. Doing so permitted her to establish relevance for the concrete lessons on claims, evidence, and reliable sources that would follow. Her intent was to expose why the learning was important by building background knowledge they could fall back on throughout this challenging unit.

While this unit lasted for multiple days, it was the first lesson in the unit when Mrs. Aguirre was laying the foundation for students to write solid pieces. The goal was to define argumentative writing and its traits. The lesson was low on the depth-of-knowledge scale, but essential to establishing sound surface-level knowledge. She wanted her students to be able to apply their understanding to develop strong arguments later.

Because she wanted them to gain a deep understanding of the connections between claims and evidence, she searched for a closure that would reveal students' learning beyond regurgitation of definitions. She asked students to represent their understanding of claims and evidence pictorially. Her experience told her that middle schoolers are usually able to make claims, but struggle more with backing them up with fact-based evidence. She wanted them to think about how these two components of argumentative writing work together. The reflection asked students to think beyond defining the terms. Image 3.3 is an example of how this learning was depicted in an analogy.

Image 3.3: Photo by Miguel Andrade on Unsplash.

She provided time for students to reflect on their understanding of claims and evidence, along with an opportunity to create a unique image. Some students drew a sketch, and others used technology. Mrs. Aguirre dedicated eight minutes to this closing task—enough to move into the next progression of learning and get students writing sooner. Her decision to use this time as a reflection to check for understanding and create a personal concept for every learner served her students and the unit well. All students now had a visual representation of their thinking to reference as they continued to learn how to write strong arguments. It proved to be time well-spent.

There is not a teacher around who cannot relate to this Hack. It's all too common to run short on time and miss a quality closure. We tend to justify the lack of cognitive summary by connecting the summary to the end of a lesson, because lessons rarely naturally button up right before the bell. Punctuating a learning time means blocking the allocated minutes, not the actual conclusion of the lesson. Keep those minutes available and home in on what the students need to do for continued productivity.

The effort to pause and sum up a mental checklist makes a person feel prepared and organized—two traits I often hear parents and teachers wishing students portrayed more regularly. Every night, I routinely punctuate my day. Put a period on that, this project gets a comma, can't wait for tomorrow when I can use the work that earned an exclamation point. When I wake, I am already a step ahead, because instead of processing what I need to accomplish today, I can recall instead. My non-caffeinated brain appreciates the lower cognitive demand first thing in the morning.

How do we ponder our daily accomplishments? The evening comes to an end even if we did not achieve all of our goals for the day. Taking the time to celebrate successes, contemplate challenges, and set goals in your class helps you put a period on your day, and is a routine that you can easily transfer to longer periods: days, weeks, and even months.

HACK 4

BE A PINBALL WIZARD

GUIDE STUDENTS TO FACILITATE
THEIR OWN CONVERSATIONS

Most people do not listen with the intent to
understand; they listen with the intent to reply.
— STEPHEN R. COVEY, EDUCATOR, AUTHOR, AND BUSINESSMAN

THE PROBLEM: TEACHERS AND STUDENTS
PLAY PING-PONG WITH QUESTIONS

ALL STUDENTS MUST have collaboration skills in order to be competent communicators. Every state expects K–12 learners to achieve a compilation of speaking and listening standards. These skills include absorbing what is heard, probing, articulating, expressing ideas clearly, and building on others' thoughts. When well-executed, these skills produce a synergic result.

Without this set of speaking and listening skills, however, the conversations feel torturous—for you and the students. When the teacher is the hub of questioning and solely responsible for maintaining a discussion, we have what I refer to as conversation ping-pong. If you go into a lesson without a plan for class discussion, you could end up with a Q&A session that looks more like the interplay between a ball and the paddles than anything truly valuable. I have seen many stellar educators lead a class discussion that they intentionally embedded into learning—but make the mistake of allowing this ping-pong game to develop.

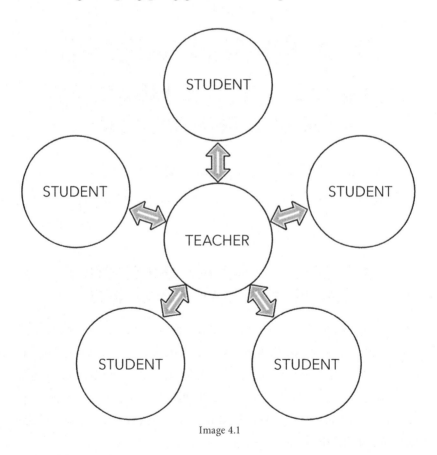

Image 4.1

It almost always starts off in the same way. A lack of verbal techniques from the students causes the teacher to jump in and kickstart the discourse. A lack of explicitly taught or planned strategies from the teacher results in them going to the standard Q&A format—and from there, to ping-pong. Notice how Image 4.1 diagrams how each conversation move includes the teacher. Few conversation moves include peers bouncing thoughts off one another.

Ping-ponging gives a false sense of discussion. Even ten exchanges generally result in the teacher contributing ten times, with ten different students contributing once, while the other fifteen to twenty students do not converse at all. Students will not improve their communication techniques by watching their teacher lead most of the discussion in the classroom. It's like playing pinball with no flippers. The pinball falls into the hole the same way dialogue halts when the teacher is not rapidly firing questions to learners in the hopes that one takes off. Ping-pong is not the strategy for successful student talk.

We need to learn to play pinball the right way, instead.

THE HACK: BE A PINBALL WIZARD

Unlike ping-pong, the traditional arcade game of pinball does not follow a back-and-forth motion. The steel ball bounces all over, triggering flashing lights, buzzers, and bells. Bumpers ricochet, launching that sphere all over the machine. Its movement varies. With a supple wrist, it can even be paused. Contact with the flipper sends it firing back up again.

All of the components of the pinball machine work together to earn points for the player. Finessing the plunger helps you control where the ball might go next. Maximizing bonuses creates musical cha-chings that cause the score to climb. Every player can use a slightly different strategy to score. The combination of multiple impacts makes you a pinball wizard.

Becoming a pinball wizard means maximizing student-to-student talk in your classroom. Achieve this objective by setting up the conditions for pinball talk moves. By this, I mean listen to students bounce their thinking off one another, rather than leading the conversation yourself. Observe as they accept challenges to intensify their learning through rich discussion. Their questions are relevant and provide clarity, connection, and respectful disagreement. They use multiple communication skills to accomplish a rich discourse.

So how do we do it?

- **Let background or prior knowledge work its magic.** People are better-equipped to respond thoughtfully to inquiry when they apply background knowledge. Too many teachers and supervising administrators have a false perspective that they should avoid surface-level questions. Without general information about a topic, though, it is impossible to debate, defend, compare/contrast, or evaluate it.

  What drains the pinball with regard to knowledge is jumping in with a high-level question and expecting students to immediately wrestle with it. It reminds me of having a conversation with my dad. He is extraordinarily intelligent and seems to know just about everything a little more deeply than I do. I'm likely to hold my own in a conversation about baking. There, I have enough experience to engage with him. Dirt, on the other hand, is a completely different situation. Al Fassezke is a self-taught horticulturist. I am no match for an intellectual conversation to determine how to create the best soil.

There will come a point in the conversation when I'm no longer able to contribute to it. I have to flip to learner mode or withdraw from the discussion.

However, debate on the value of homework? Bring it on! My background knowledge, experiences, and established beliefs about homework can be challenged and I am in a position to defend them. Evidence, data, pitfalls, and even research are at my fingertips and ready to share. Justifying my opinions and backing them up is a cognitively stimulating conversation, one filled with questions that fuel the fire.

Students can work their wizardry when they have tools like academic vocabulary, relevant experiences, and resources that support their thinking and learning during their pinball talk.

In the classroom, this equates to teachers posing questions way above students' heads without giving them the tools to do the questions justice. In many cases, they are not bad questions. Rather, teachers expect them to generate a rich discussion—but too soon in the learning progression. In the absence of experience or knowledge, the students lack true answers, and they quickly exhaust the conversation. Either heavy scaffolding turns into spoon-feeding, or the project morphs into an experience that produces a lower level of learning than expected.

Avoid this stall in your pinball talk by fueling their talk with sufficient background knowledge or common experiences. Students can work their wizardry when they have tools like academic vocabulary, relevant experiences, and resources that support their thinking and learning during their pinball talk.

• **Encourage active listening.** Since listening is tough to assess, we frequently overlook it. Listening is typically referenced in classrooms as a behavior expectation for when the teacher is talking. Oodles of posters are displayed in elementary classrooms depicting good listeners who can "gimme five." But from the onset of their education, students learn that listening is about what their eyes, ears, mouths, hands, and feet are doing, without a reference to what their brains are doing. In the absence of explicit guidance about what excellent listeners are thinking, students interpret it as "be quiet and be still."

This is a behavior expectation for being a good audience member. It does not teach students to be active listeners. Active listeners interact with the speaker to gain clarity, probe, and paraphrase.

I'm convinced that listening is the most undervalued communication skill. In order for a class discussion to look like a pinball in action, make sure you're keeping the emphasis on more than just talk. Ask for feedback, check in with students, and lead discussions that measure how well they're listening. Active listeners give their attention to the speaker's message with the purpose of understanding or connecting to it. If you want a discussion to be engaging, purposeful, and effective, build an atmosphere where quality listening plays a vital role.

- **Emphasize the value of alternate perspectives.** Argument and debate can be very productive methods of learning. Considering points of view that differ from your own not only deepens your understanding of the topic, but it also opens doors to exploring new ways of thinking. This mindset of inquiry fosters a desire to grow. Entering a conversation with a single viewpoint and a determination to be right is detrimental to everyone's learning. This often escalates emotions. If emotions overpower the message, the conversation sours and becomes unproductive to learning. Set the tone for an expansion of thinking to be the purpose of dialogue, rather than being right or wrong. Doing so sustains a pinball structure where students can agree, build on one another, or challenge thoughts without triggering defense mechanisms.

- **Develop a command of language to articulate thinking.** Speaker and listener have to work together to create a dialogue, because dialogue and discussion require all parties to speak well. Teach students how to accomplish good speech with the following tips to encourage pinball wizardry in your classroom:

- Vary pitch; avoid a monotone voice.

- Adjust rate of speech, speeding up or slowing down to communicate emotion or emphasize a word or phrase.

- Pause and intentionally place moments of silence in the dialogue to allow the listener to process a key point or bring attention to something the speaker just said.

- Adjust sentence structure to bring attention to the message, or risk losing the audience. Multiple lengthy sentences are more challenging to follow. Short, fragmented sentences used too frequently can sound overly simplistic.

- Volume. It is impossible to create a pinball structure if the speakers cannot be heard. If students are too soft-spoken, their contributions are drained.

Providing sufficient time for students to think and prepare for a conversation is another way to support their command of language. With a bit of planning and an opportunity to process a thought, they can determine what to communicate and then craft the delivery of that idea in a way that can be easily understood.

- **Notice and respond to social cues.** Strategizing how words are delivered is a large part of being a competent communicator. Be mindful of how the audience receives the thought so you can keep the conversation on track. Listeners give signs that can help the speaker

figure out when to repeat, clarify, check for understanding, or pause to let the audience chew on something. Speakers can interpret head shakes, loss of eye
contact, tightening of lips, sighing, or frowns as indi-
cations that they need to make an adjustment to their
talks. Help students understand these cues so they can
respond to them during their pinball talk. Image 4.2
provides a visual representation of how to diagram pinball conversations. Use your wizardry to remove yourself from your students' conversations, and hand over
the controls to let students bounce off one another.

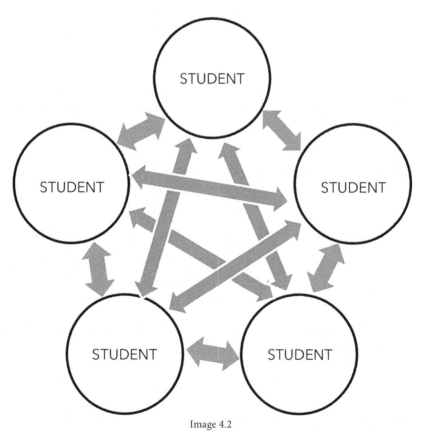

Image 4.2

WHAT YOU CAN DO TOMORROW

Since we are speaking and listening all the time, we always have opportunities to focus on skills that will help class discussion move away from ping-pong and look more like pinball.

- **Delineate good listeners from good audience members.** If you address listening skills in your classroom, verify that the skills you're teaching foster collaboration and productive speaking and listening. Set guidelines for being a captive audience. Students receive mixed messages if we tell them good listeners are quiet. Good audience members are quiet, but active listeners offer words of encouragement, post clarifying questions, and build on the speaker's words. When a speaker is presenting, tell the rest of the class that they're the audience members.

  When the speaker is taking a turn at dialogue, encourage the other students to use their active listening tools. Presentations have audience members. Collaborative conversations have active listeners. Prompting students

to be good audience members when they are working in groups can discourage dialogue.

Just because traits of active listeners and good audience members overlap, like avoiding distracting gestures and thinking about the message, does not mean they are the same in all ways. In order to have pinball conversations, students must use active listening, not simply watch the show.

- **Square up.** This is a powerful strategy to bring attention to the speaker. Instructing students to "square up" means that their shoulders are squarely facing the speaker. By positioning their shoulders in the direction of the person talking, they naturally look at the speaker. Using this strategy is particularly helpful if you notice the audience getting distracted by peers, objects, or other work.

- **Model accurate paraphrasing.** Emphasis on *accurate*. Students can organically practice their abilities to deliver clear messages throughout their day. We can fall into the trap of building onto a student's thoughts by putting the words we wish they had said into our paraphrase. Instead of inserting accurate vocabulary or elaborating on a spawning idea, let the student hear what you heard by repeating only what the student actually said. Listen for clues like, "What I think you meant was ..." That is a springboard for embellishing the student's words with what you wish they would have said. If a portion of the response is unclear and needs elaboration, ask for it rather than providing it. Doing so benefits the speaker and models how to use questioning to seek understanding.

- **Narrate social cues.** What might be obvious to you could be completely missed by others. Labeling what you notice as you look around the room brings attention to the messages students send to a speaker—and these messages affect the discussion. Teachers observe these cues almost subconsciously. It might require extra concentration and mindfulness to bring these cues to light, but it's an important part of teaching your students to be observant when they're in the middle of a discussion. Preface your reasoning for a decision by sharing your observations. Here are examples:

  - I see that some of you are looking confused.
  - Your face suggests that I haven't been clear.
  - All this murmuring tells me you have something to say.
  - It's easy to see that you are ready to go.

- Seems like your brain is distracted by something else.

Once you narrate the cause for your action, follow up with how that observation impacted your thoughts as a speaker.

- Your face suggests that I haven't been clear. Let me try sharing it in a different way.

- All this murmuring tells me you have something to say. Turn and ask your partners to give their thoughts so you can share your thinking before we continue.

- **Start with ABC.** As a transition to using pinball talk moves, start with three basic connecting

CAUTION: ASKING, "DOES ANYONE WANT TO AGREE, BUILD ON, OR CHALLENGE RILEY'S COMMENT?" TURNS THE PINBALL CONVERSATION BETWEEN STUDENTS INTO A PING-PONG CONVERSATION THAT FOCUSES ON YOU. INSTEAD, USE VISUALS LIKE A POSTER (SEE APPENDIX) AND REFERENCE IT WITH A SILENT CUE.

phrases. Mrs. Kate Budzinski, a fourth-grade teacher, encourages students to avoid ping-ponging the conversation back to her by silently cueing students to use ABC in their discussion.

- **Agree:** I agree because …
- **Build:** I would like to build on that by adding …
- **Challenge:** I have a challenge to your thinking…

- **Communicate social goals.** Rarely is there a lesson plan without a content goal. During portions of class time when students are using their social skills, consider drawing their attention to a specific social goal. It makes sense to highlight speaking and listening skills, but move beyond the obvious and alert students to the social skills that could immediately improve their collaboration time. Use your observations from previous peer interactions to pinpoint the social goal, which could be:

  - Equalizing talk time
  - Exhausting all ideas
  - Encouraging others to share
  - Making it productive, not personal
  - Checking for everyone's understanding

- Building a process for making decisions when there is disagreement
- Probing with questions
- Asking open-ended questions
- Using evidence to support your idea
- Applying academic vocabulary in your conversations

A BLUEPRINT FOR FULL IMPLEMENTATION

Step 1: Get the K–12 picture of speaking and listening skills.

One anchor standard from the Common Core State Standards reads: *Prepare for and participate effectively in a range of conversations and collaborations with diverse partners, building on others' ideas and expressing their own clearly and persuasively.* The anchor standard is the foundation to which each grade-level standard aligns. Year after year, students develop a progression of skills and strategies on their journeys toward this overarching goal. Teachers find it enlightening to see how the standards build each year. Noting where they overlap and where new components are introduced helps teachers see what students have already been expected to do and what learning is new to them. With this clarity, teachers can make instructional decisions to address activating prior knowledge or introducing something new.

In about fifteen to twenty minutes, a small group of educators can vertically view all K–12 standards in a specific strand. The process is simple and it's an efficient way to get a big picture of a student's thirteen years of school. Begin by organizing the standards by strand, not by grade. Putting an entire strand in a single document saves time. Provide everyone with a copy of the document and follow these steps:

1. Begin with kindergarten. Read the standard and discuss its meaning to be sure everyone understands what success in this standard will look like.

2. Move to first grade. Compare and contrast first grade and kindergarten. Highlight the parts of the first-grade standard that were not present in kindergarten. This is the new learning, and isolates what first-graders will be learning.

3. Continue to follow this process for the standards for each year through grade twelve. This is not a highlighting activity; it is a compare/contrast task. To glean

> WHEN WORDS SEEM TO BE SYNONYMS BUT ARE CHANGED FROM GRADE TO GRADE, DO NOT ASSUME THEY MEAN THE SAME THING. THE AUTHORS OF THE STANDARDS INTENTIONALLY CHOSE EACH VERB WITH ITS DISTINCT MEANING. IT IS CRITICAL TO ARTICULATE HOW EACH IS UNIQUE.

the most from this protocol, discuss things with your peers. Through your talk, you will gain perspective on where the learners in your class have been, should be, and will go in their speaking and listening skills.

4. Now you have a bird's eye view of the vertical progression. Use this perspective as you revisit the standard that represents the age group you work with most closely. Teachers who engage in this task will have a solid grasp on the skills they teach. The lens of seeing a piece to the full puzzle showcases how important it is to address these skills every year.

Step 2: Perform a crosswalk of grade-level standards and student performance.

After you have a clear picture of what your state expects, observe students in action. Conduct a crosswalk to compare the standards with the pinball talk used in collaborative environments. Use these guiding questions to help analyze your observations:

- How do they engage in dialogue?

- What are the commonalities between successful talks that pinball effortlessly? What patterns can you find in conversations that are less productive?

- Where students need growth, are the patterns in areas that are teacher-directed? If so, modify how you are engaging in the lesson. Be objective about this one.

- As the teacher becomes more invisible, are students accessing communication skills that create pinball talks?

- What skills are evident and naturally executed by students, and which ones are still lacking?

Use your findings to prioritize the communication skills that are likely to provide the biggest bang for your buck. Suppose your anecdotal evidence suggests that students are not proficient in actively listening. Take time to teach and practice active listening so students can transfer it to their pinball talk.

Step 3: Set paraphrasing as a norm.

The communication cycle consists of both listening and speaking. Most students concentrate on the speaking side of that cycle. Teaching students to summarize what they heard in the form of a paraphrase accomplishes multiple goals. First, it ensures that the listener is actually listening and not simply waiting for a turn to talk. Second, it validates that the listener heard it accurately. Recapping the statement gives the initial speaker an opportunity to clarify any gaps and confirm the message was received as intended.

WARN STUDENTS TO AVOID THESE PARA- PHRASING PITFALLS: #1: THE PARAPHRASE IS LONGER THAN WHAT WAS SAID. #2: THE LIS- TENER PARAPHRASES TOO OFTEN. #3: THE PARAPHRASE IS PARROTING EXACTLY WHAT WAS SAID.

Paraphrasing also helps keep the conversation on topic. Students are more likely to comment about what was said when they paraphrase it first, as opposed to taking the group in a different direction. Finally, when the listener para- phrases what the first speaker said, the first speaker is interested. It helps to increase the amount of time students can focus on what another peer has to say, which sets the stage for pinball talk moves.

Step 4: Carefully choose your protocols.

As a teacher, you have a number of protocols available to you for organizing collaboration. Choosing the right one can mean the difference between productive group work and a management nightmare. Select your protocols based on various criteria. The most important one is to complete an academic task related to the content learning target. To double dip on your outcome, choose a protocol that also builds a needed social skill during the learning. To get you started, use Image 4.3 to learn to coordinate social skills to address, and to learn what details to look for in a protocol. The image also provides examples of protocols that align. Use it as a springboard!

Problem	Protocol Traits to Help	Suggestions
One student monopolizes the conversation	• Silent routines • Timed rotations	• Chalk Talk • Final Word
Answer getting without reflection	• Structured questioning	• Reciprocal Teaching
Some students do not participate equally	• Independent tasks	• Jigsaw • Round Table Discussion
Limited ideas or perspectives	• Brainstorming	• Give One – Get One • Speed Dating

Image 4.3

Step 5: Collect data and share feedback on collaborative conversations.

You cannot cast a magic spell upon your students to transform them into expert pinballers. Students need to practice and reflect on how they are becoming pinball wizards themselves. As your students work together, gather evidence about how they are using the needed social skills to execute pinball talk. Punctuate the lesson by reflecting on their teamwork in addition to or instead of a reflection on content. Then, collect their perspectives and compare them to your notes. This consistency check between your observations and theirs opens the door to see how they used their communication skills.

Offer feedback to individual students on their use of the targeted social skill, too. Before launching them into the next collaborative task, invite them to identify something that will help their group be more productive together. Encourage them to use the feedback they received to set goals and determine how well they did. Bringing them into the game will transform them into owning their own learning.

OVERCOMING PUSHBACK

Talking yourself into keeping a ping-pong approach will make you work harder while allowing students to sit back and relax, physically and mentally. Following are common worries that lend themselves to abandoning the drive to have a rich discourse:

When students are asked to clarify, sometimes they don't know how. This pushback has two parts. The first refers back to Hack 2: Kick the IDK Bucket. If you suspect that students don't know something, it is important to determine whether they really don't know or if there is another reason they are not responding. When students give incomplete responses and have trouble clarifying, it gives you a perfect opportunity to model how to use a pinball strategy. Try the same ABC system shared in What You Can Do Tomorrow. If you are going to build on a student's response, do not paraphrase it with "I think what you mean is…" In order to establish a culture of inquiry and learning together, building on someone's idea should become commonplace. Take the opportunity to provide a quality example by quoting the sentence stem verbatim: "I would like to build on what ____ said." Model. Model. Model.

By the time they get to my grade, they should already know how to collaborate. Enhancing collaboration skills does not have an endpoint. As adults, we continue to sharpen our skills and improve our abilities to work with others. It's a limiting idea that there is a cutoff to when students should master communicating with others. Like any academic skill, if students are lacking in an area, we should provide interventions, supports, and quality instruction to help them catch up. The "guess you should have paid attention last year" mentality does no justice to students, and does not help the level of harmonious learning in your space.

It is hard to hold everyone's attention in a whole-class discussion. This is especially true if the teacher looks at the lack of engaging conversations as a classroom-management problem. Smaller collaborative learning groups exist for precisely this reason. Teams with fewer members offer a greater opportunity for equal input and consensus-building. Easing into longer periods of time is another way to transition into lengthy talks. Start with a few minutes and work your way up.

If they don't raise their hands, everyone will talk at once. At a very young age, students learn to manage conversations in social settings. This ability to execute skills such as listening for a lull before interjecting is an experience they bring with them to the classroom. Students who talk over one another in the lunchroom are commonly told by their peers to "be quiet." Be slow to interject when multiple students begin to speak. It will give them the opportunity to facilitate their own pinball conversation. A nudge to draw their attention to the problem permits them a second opportunity to monitor themselves and apply their active listening.

THE HACK IN ACTION

In early September, sixth-grade teacher Mrs. Elizabeth Brownell invited a group of fellow teachers and me into her classroom. Being so early in the year, she was still setting expectations for her middle schoolers. We wanted to see her process for teaching them how to engage in conversation. Mrs. Brownell is an English Language Arts teacher who frequently uses Turn and Asks or Think-Pair-Shares in her classroom, which includes a high population of English language learners. Mrs. Brownell consistently is mindful of the importance of explicitly teaching students how to engage in speaking and listening skills. Even though middle schoolers are social creatures, their dialogue is often limited to themselves and their lives outside the classroom—unless they are taught how to use talk in academic settings.

In this specific lesson, our observations focused on listening. The lesson started with a video clip from the popular sitcom *The Big Bang Theory*. In the clip, Sheldon and Amy are having dinner. Sheldon is telling Amy about different gaming systems. Amy wants him to pass the butter. Sheldon continues talking about video games and accuses Amy of not listening. Amy then promises to give Sheldon her undivided attention.

The video was less than two minutes long, and students were told they would be watching it twice. The first time to get the gist and the second time to look for a specific intention. Mrs. Brownell purposefully withheld the guiding question until the second viewing. After the first video run, she asked, "Who is the better listener?" After a brief pause for think time, she triggered a response and the students replied "Amy" in unison. This is a simple question, and important to establish before moving into gathering evidence. Mrs. Brownell then displayed the guiding question on the board. "What evidence did you observe that tells you Amy was an effective listener?"

Before playing the clip again, she instructed students to repeat the question they were trying to answer. In this lesson, students had a visual of the question on the board, so she had them read it for themselves. In other lessons, I have observed her telling students to repeat the question to their partners. The motive for repeating the question is to make sure students heard and are focused on why they are watching the clip. It brings emphasis to the purpose, and will likely reduce the number of comments that do not relate to the learning target.

Students began listing observable traits that align with active listening. The application task for this lesson gave students multiple opportunities to practice the main skill Mrs. Brownell was teaching: paraphrasing. In September, she devoted an entire class period to teaching students to be excellent paraphrasers, so she could establish that as an expectation for all future protocols. Embedding the ability for students to paraphrase sets her up to be invisible more often for the rest of the year.

Fast forward to spring of the same school year. Paraphrasing is now a norm in Mrs. Brownell's classroom. Before students agree/

disagree with one another, they paraphrase what they are referencing. Here are a few examples:

- When you said (insert paraphrase), it reminded me of …

- Your comment (insert paraphrase) gives me another question.

- I was a bit unclear when you said (insert paraphrase). What did you mean by that?

- I agree with you when you said (insert paraphrase).

- Your point about (insert paraphrase) conflicts with my idea because …

These students have not only been taught how to paraphrase; they could effectively prepare questions for discussion and challenge one another's claims with respectful discourse. Mrs. Brownell's students are able to have less ping-pong with her and more pinball talk with each other.

Some choose to point the finger at technology and social media for diminishing the quality of conversations in which today's children partake. It is true that tone, prose, and emotion are left up to interpretation when communication is shared via email or text. Perhaps today's method of talk does impact the quality of verbal interactions, yet the ability for students to initiate, maintain, and expand their dialogue with one another remains an academic priority—one that is unequivocally relevant in life.

One approach to solving this problem is to implement Hack 1: Assume All Hands Are Up. The strategies in Hack 1 are intended to address an engagement issue. This Hack, on the other hand, addresses a communication issue. Whipping out KleenSlates or throwing in a paper exit ticket will increase the number of students who participate in the lesson ... but do very little to develop or refine their communication skills so they learn to listen with the intent to understand.

Watch for conversations to follow a pinball approach rather than a ping-pong volley. The more time you spend sharpening students' speaking and listening skills, the better communicators they will become, and the more pinballing you can do in your classroom. Employers are seeking competent communicators, collaborative thinkers, and contributing team members. These are truly life skills that will serve your students as they grow older.

HACK 5

PLAY THE BROKEN RECORD
REPLAY QUESTIONS TO MAINTAIN FOCUS

*Any idea, plan, or purpose may be placed in
the mind through repetition of thought.*
— NAPOLEON HILL, AMERICAN AUTHOR

THE PROBLEM: THERE ARE TOO MANY
QUESTIONS TO PLAN THEM ALL

TEACHERS ASK AN average of fifty to one hundred questions per hour. Teachers of all grade levels and content areas fit in this range. Most educators are surprised to find they ask this many questions and would estimate the number to be closer to ten or twenty. What surprises me about this is that the teachers I have observed are aware that we are tallying the questions they ask. Their reactions when they hear that they posed 124 questions to students are best described as disbelief. Their shock at the number of questions tells me one thing: They are not consciously thinking about what questions they're asking. They can't even remember they asked a question at all, let alone what the question was.

It's overwhelming to take on the responsibility of planning that many different questions. I'd go so far as to say it's unreasonable. As a result, most teachers often "go with the flow" of the lesson and spend little to no time planning questions in advance. It is challenging to do it on the fly, though, and that creates a number of problems, including:

- Divergent questions
- Questions repeatedly rephrased without releasing each one to students
- Poorly articulated or confusing questions
- Partially asked questions
- Teachers answering their own questions

The fact that so many teachers are oblivious to how many questions they're asking means they're also unaware of the impact they have on triggering student thought. Take the notion of five hundred or more questions floating in and out of students' ears on any given school day.

How are students expected to decipher which questions are the most representative of the lesson's purpose? You might be inclined to think all of the questions are important. In a sense, they are.

However, if a teacher doesn't give merit to a certain question over another, students perceive that all questions are equally relevant. This is not true. Some questions are tightly aligned to the lesson, some are loosely aligned, some offer a thought path to get to the learning point, and some questions are, frankly, irrelevant.

When the teacher loses sight of the purpose of the lesson and unintentionally runs with a nugget of student interest rather than sticking to the topic, it increases the potential for learning gaps. You can spiral into question after nuanced question and lose your focus on the lesson itself. In the end, you wind up far from the beginning, and don't remember how you got there.

Let me emphasize the point that the problem is *unintentionally* diverting from a lesson plan. Often, it is a wise decision to consciously choose to divert for various reasons, but it is an instructional decision. You should not be surprised at the end of the class time that the topic took a different path. This leads to confused students who feel like they didn't learn anything in school today.

Instead of allowing ourselves—and our students—to become overwhelmed by the number of questions, and allowing those questions to spiral out of control, we need to become more intentional with the questions we ask, and how we design them.

THE HACK: PLAY THE BROKEN RECORD

Don't worry: The answer isn't to script out one hundred questions and ask them all in order. The solution is much simpler and more manageable. Playing the Broken Record means that you formulate a few key questions. These questions provide you with consistent data on how students are progressing, and drive home the purpose for learning. Revisit that core group of questions from multiple angles several times within the lesson. Each time you return to the key questions, you are playing the Broken Record.

For those of you who never owned a record player, let me share the origin of the simile used when something sounds like a "broken record." Before iTunes, MP3s, CDs, or even cassette tapes, people purchased music on vinyl records that required a record player to hear them. A needle ran along grooves in the record, creating vibrations, and these vibrations were transferred into sound through an amplifier. All this worked just fine unless there was a scratch or any damage to the record. A scratch would cause the record to skip. The needle passed over segments of the song, omitting notes or multiple measures at a time. A more common result of a scratched record was that it jumped backward and repeated short clips of the record. These repetitions would continue until the listener manually moved the needle past the scratch so the music would play on.

Decide which questions will trigger or assess learning, and go back to them over and over.

Clearly, it is nonsensical to plan every question. Far too many variables make that impossible or even impractical. A more reasonable approach is to determine what questions you *do* need to plan and use them as your Broken Record questions.

Decide which questions will trigger or assess learning, and go back to them over and over. This accomplishes several goals. One, it keeps you—and the lesson—on track. This isn't to say that you should discourage natural curiosity in students, and the rabbit holes it might take us down. We want to cultivate natural curiosity in students. But that interest should not take you so far away from the lesson's purpose that the lesson itself gets lost. Playing the Broken Record reinforces the main purpose of learning. Sure, unintended learning points often appear in any lesson, but those are bonuses. They do not replace the learning target, which is the lesson focus. Playing the Broken Record serves as a reminder for students of the big idea around learning, and brings you back around to the lesson if you get off track.

In Ms. Jennifer A. Corrado's second-grade classroom, students were learning how to use observation to classify objects into different groups. She started by modeling this concept with a collection of her son's (clean) socks. During the focus lesson, she set the stage for the questions students were going to hear (repeatedly) during their collaborative learning time. She chose a pair of Broken Record questions to link observation and the act of using that observation to sort or classify:

1. What do you observe/see/notice?

2. How can you use that to classify the sock into a group?

The progression of her questions always comes back to these two big ideas: giving students a process they could count on, and bringing them back to the teacher's expectations for what they should be learning during the lesson.

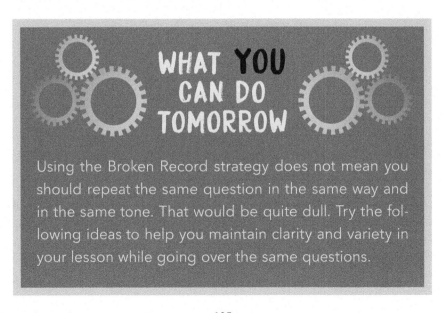

WHAT YOU CAN DO TOMORROW

Using the Broken Record strategy does not mean you should repeat the same question in the same way and in the same tone. That would be quite dull. Try the following ideas to help you maintain clarity and variety in your lesson while going over the same questions.

Learning Target	Question(s)
SS: Describe the connection between the three branches of government.	What is the connection between the three branches of government?
Spanish: Use the present tense of the -ar verbs cocinar (to cook), preparar (to prepare) and lavar (to wash) to speak about what you and others do in the kitchen.	¿Qué cocinas? (What do you cook?) ¿Qué cocina? (What does he/she cook?) ¿Qué preparas? (What do you prepare?) ¿Qué prepara? (What does he/she prepare?) ¿Qué lavas? (What do you wash?) ¿Qué lava? (What does he/she wash?)
ELA: Identify the author's message in a story.	What is the author trying to tell us? Why did the author write this story?
PE: Use chasing tactics in tag games.	What tactic are you using? How/When is that tactic effective? What other tactics could you use?
Math: Compare two functions that are each represented differently.	How does this graph and this expression compare to one another? How is the expression represented in the graph?
Music: Read, define, and demonstrate the use of staccato.	What does this articulation tell you? What does this articulation mean? How would you play these notes using the staccato articulation?
Art: Use various techniques to create an illusion of depth.	How did you create depth? Why did you choose overlapping/placement/size to create depth?

Image 5.1

- **Turn your learning target into a question.** This might be the easiest strategy in the entire book. It is so simple to flip a statement into a question—which will then engage the students and get their brains moving. The table in Image 5.1 offers content examples of how teachers turned their learning targets into Broken Record questions. What better way to bring attention to the learning target than to ask about it specifically?

- **Test your consistency.** When you play the Broken Record, your line of questions might become predictable. A benefit of students being able to anticipate what you will ask is that it allows them to build a self-checking process. As you approach a conversation with a student about his or her progress, try starting out by asking, "What's the first question I am going to ask you?" If the student is able to guess at a question that directly aligns with the learning target, you will know they have used your past questions to figure out this lesson's purpose.

- **Use questions for content. Use statements for expectations.** You can draw attention to your questions by reducing the number of them. Consider using statements or requests for prompting students to comply with your expectations. Instead of asking, "Do you have your name on your paper?" simply say, "Check to see if your name is on your paper." If you are trying to teach students to follow a procedure and you don't want to continually remind them, the statement can be more nuanced: "Be sure your paper has complete and proper formatting."

- **Craft questions that accurately represent your learning target.** It matters not if you craft a question that connects to your learning target, or develop one with students. Either way, throughout the lesson, use that question to help students maintain their focus. Find a lead that feels comfortable and not artificial to you. Here are examples for a learning target that reads: *Identify strategies that help readers determine the main idea of an informational text.*

  - What is a strategy readers can use to determine the main idea of this text?

  - What different strategy can readers use to determine the main idea of this text?

  - What strategy did you use to figure out the main idea?

  - What did the author do to help readers determine the main idea of this text?

  The focus in the learning target is for students to describe *how* they determined the main idea, not *what* the main idea is. Forming a question around that allows students to start from the correct point, and repeating that question brings them back to the idea again and again.

During a sequence of questioning, it might be necessary to beg the obvious question: "What is the main idea of this text?" The problem is that the answer to that question does not provide evidence that the student has met the learning target. Identifying the main idea might be a starting point for assisting learners in describing the strategy they used to conclude it. It is not an ending point that qualifies it as a Broken Record because it does not do the learning target justice.

Using the question, "What is the main idea of this text?" changes the thought process altogether. Even if students can identify the main idea, it does not mean they can articulate *how* it was determined—let alone in multiple ways, as the learning target asks. One of the options in this lesson is the Broken Record question. It might be helpful to go on a cognitive walk with students through the process of identifying the main idea. When choosing a Broken Record question, you will have to ensure that the cognitive walk circles back to the main idea of the lesson (pun intended).

A BLUEPRINT FOR FULL IMPLEMENTATION

Step 1: Review your lesson plan and identify the essence of what students will learn.

Broken Record questions align with what students are learning. Remember that teaching and learning are not synonyms. Few teachers walk into a lesson without an idea of what they will be *teaching*. The lessons that produce results are planned with learning in mind, not teaching in mind. For example, a teacher might say she is teaching about the heart. This is a topic, not a learning target. The learning affiliated with a lesson within a health unit on the heart might be to monitor and adjust physical activity to stay within a target heart rate. That is your learning goal. Using an intention for learning like this offers the teacher direction in developing relevant Broken Record questions.

Step 2: Picture the cognitive walk students will take to meet today's learning target.

Building on knowledge that students already have expedites understanding. Therefore, for the effectiveness of the lesson, it is critical to know the sequence of logical steps that will lead to learning. Using the previous learning goal from step one, adjust for background knowledge that you will either need to access or provide.

Learning target: Monitor and adjust physical activity to stay within a target heart rate.

In order to achieve this, students will have to know how to do the following:

- Determine target heart rate.

- Measure heart rate.

- Identify ways to increase/decrease heart rate.

If students do not have these skills, they will have difficulty learning the target. Now you have developed a sequence of learning progressions that you can use to intentionally select your Broken Record questions.

Step 3: Flip the learning progressions into big questions.

These big questions will help you and your students determine if they have the necessary understanding to tackle the full learning target. Break down your overall goal for the day into sizable chunks that are necessary for success. These become your Broken Record questions, and are good candidates for formative assessment.

- What is the target heart rate?

- How is the heart rate measured?

- What types of physical activities increase/decrease heart rate?

It can be helpful to modify these Broken Record questions in ways that do not change the focus or lower the level of the questions. For example:

- What kind of exercise increases/decreases your heart rate?

- What is one way to increase your heart rate?

- What can you do to make your heart rate go up?

- If you wanted to slow down your heart rate, what could you do?

Step 4: Collect formative assessment data on the big questions.

Responses to questions will expose what students understand and what they have not grasped yet. Exit tickets seem to have become the universal tool for gathering formative data, but it is important to recognize that formative assessment is more than just another activity for students to complete. Formative assessment done well is intentional. In step three of this Hack, you have broken down the components of the lesson. If students are unable to meet the learning target (monitor and adjust physical activity to stay within their target heart rate), but you don't assess learning until the end of the lesson, it means that you don't know where the students stopped learning.

Even though experienced teachers can be accurate in their predictions about what students might have found difficult, still, guesswork is involved. Take the guesswork out of the equation by using your Broken Record questions to intentionally collect formative data on each of the pieces to the learning puzzle. If a student can tell you how to determine a heart rate, but not how to adjust it, you have an open door that wouldn't have existed without that data. Organize students depending on where they are running up against a barrier, and you'll be able to help with purpose. Think of all the instructional time you'll save when you can be deliberate with whom and what you reteach. This beats repeating the entire lesson, by a longshot!

Your Broken Record questions have just increased the learning the students will do, increased your data collection, and decreased your reteaching time. And all while keeping your lesson on track.

Step 5: Close the lesson with the Broken Record questions.

The brain processes information in reverse. The last thing students engage in, cognitively speaking, is most likely to be recalled first. Feel free to test this out. Give someone a verbal list of five events in the near future that are posted on your calendar. After you share your list, ask them to repeat the list. The last event you listed will likely be the first one they remember. After that, since relevance is important, their memory will hold onto anything on your list that they connected to. And then they might be at a loss for what the rest of the list contained.

The point is that we can help students retain information by taking advantage of this understanding. Even if your lesson runs long and you do not complete everything you had planned, close the lesson by returning to the Broken Record question that aligns to the learning target. You might find students recognizing that they still have work to do to achieve the learning goal, or seeing that they truly have a handle on the learning. Either way, this conclusion allows them to reflect on where they are in their learning journey, identify what they still need to do to get there, and make themselves part of the plan that makes it happen. You are giving them ownership of their learning. (See Hack 3: Punctuate Your Learning Time, for more on concluding a lesson.)

OVERCOMING PUSHBACK

Sadly, most educators are not accustomed to strategies that reduce the workload. So some teachers might feel like this Broken Record questioning is taking the easy way out. It is not about less effort, though. It is about shifting that effort from teachers to students. The answer to that piece of pushback is simple: We're Hacking you out of thinking on your feet so often!

Aren't I supposed to see where the lesson takes us? Exploring student wonderings triggered by new ideas and perspectives is exciting for both students and teachers. We want to encourage and model how to follow a natural path of thought. However, the lack of clarity in a lesson is education suicide. Without a clear goal for what students will learn, you create gaps in their learning. It's like taking a road trip to your cousin's wedding in another state. You can stop along the way to tour the countryside—as long as you don't get lost and miss the wedding as a result.

What about science and driving questions? Even easier! Oftentimes, the driving question *is* the Broken Record question. It's not necessary to flip the learning target. Try adding a reflection to your driving question to keep students on track.

- How is this helping you answer the driving question?
- What does that tell you about the driving question?
- How might this connect to the driving question?
- What information do you have that will help you respond to the driving question?

If I keep asking the same question, students will keep repeating the same answers. Do you ever find yourself saying, "That's what I've been saying"? If not to your students, to your principal, your partner, or your own children? It's often necessary for someone to hear something multiple times before they have a deep understanding of it. This is especially true when the new information is mixed in with other new ideas. If you can reveal a consistent pattern through Broken Record questioning, students can begin to see truths about content.

THE HACK IN ACTION

Mrs. Mary Steinberg's Algebra II class hosted a CIFT lesson on a day when students were learning the difference between theoretical and experimental probability. Before the lesson, Mrs. Steinberg shared her plan with the team. She explained that she wanted students to learn how and why theoretical and experimental probability were different. This was an introductory lesson, and she needed students to have a sound understanding of these two concepts before going deeper into statistics.

She explained that students should know the difference from seventh grade, but based on a formative assessment from yesterday, she needed to do a refresher on the definitions of each. Instead of giving a boring lecture, she wanted to trigger their prior knowledge of the vocabulary while launching them into a wondering of why these ideas were not the same. She also sought to sharpen their collaboration skills by asking them to work as a team. Since she expected students to grasp the actual mathematics fairly quickly, she used this opportunity to build learning teams that worked together productively.

The lesson included students using a pack of Skittles to calculate the theoretical probability. If they pulled out a piece of candy from the packet without looking at it, what were the chances that it would be a specific color? This was the first step in the learning progression. Mrs. Steinberg was keenly aware that students would not be able to compare/contrast or apply their understanding of probability to future statistics lessons if they couldn't even provide a definition and an example—including completing the calculations.

She asked them to make their calculations independently, then compare their answers with a partner. As they compared their answers, she asked many questions, though every pair of students had one question in common. Why are your answers different for the same color? When students could explain that not all packs had the same number of candies, and that most partners had different numbers of each color, and that this meant the probability of choosing an orange Skittle was 20 percent for one partner and 29 percent for another, she knew she was getting somewhere. Another group had one partner who calculated a 0 percent. Mrs. Steinberg systematically approached every table and documented whether students provided evidence that they could define theoretical probability, and whether they could use mathematical reasoning to explain why their partners calculated the same or different chances.

Next, she posed a question to the entire class: How sure are you that your calculations are accurate? All students were confident in their answers. So she followed up by asking them how they could prove it by testing their calculations. They had discussions at their tables about how many trials they would need to do to "prove" their calculations. She listened as students' confidence slowly diminished. The more they talked, the less confident they were in their calculations. Some groups wanted a range of percentages, while other groups wanted unlimited trials until the percentage matched up. She was beginning to see them struggle with using experimental methods to prove the theoretical probability.

Before they got frustrated, she allowed each of them to identify the conditions of the experiment, then test the data. She again used Broken Record questioning. She asked every table various questions, but made one inquiry to every table: How did your experimental results compare to your theoretical calculations? She then followed up the question with: Why? Some groups needed additional prompts, but in the end, she asked the same question to all students and rated their responses and justifications on a documentation chart she carried around. The chart indicated whether they were able to articulate the reasoning using mathematical vocabulary, were able to explain it using what she called "teen talk," or were not able to provide a logical explanation for why the results were not the same.

During the lesson, she asked the following questions one to three times:

- Are possibility and chance the same thing?

- Are there different possible outcomes?

- Do you have control over the outcomes?

- What's the next step?

- What does that mean?

- How do you calculate the percentage?

- Did you do your calculations already?

- What do you predict will happen?

- Why did Sage use the word "should" when she said that's what *should* happen?

- After you pick a color, what do you do with that candy? Keep it out or put it back in the pack?

- How will you determine how many trials are enough?

- What were the outcomes of your Skittle experiment?

- Where does probability fit in a teacher's world?

- What other careers rely on probability?

- How sure are you?

She asked the following questions more than five times each in a class of twenty-five students:

- Is that the same as your theoretical calculation? (six)

- What do you think? (ten)

- Did anything surprise you? (seventeen)

- How did your experimental results compare to your theoretical calculations? (twenty-five)

- How can you prove it? (twenty-six)

- Why? (thirty-five)

While some of the questions were prompts to get the students thinking more generally, they make it clear what the lesson was focused on. To close the lesson, and before the exit ticket, Mrs. Steinberg invited students to enjoy their Skittles. She explained that it is impolite to talk with food in your mouth, so she was going to give them something to chew on, both figuratively and literally. What was the purpose of this lesson? What did they think they were supposed to learn today?

After a brief quiet time for thinking (and chewing), she asked them to share their predictions for the learning target with their partners. Mrs. Steinberg positioned herself to stand and listen in on two different partner groups. We later learned when we debriefed the lesson that three out of four of those students did not provide sufficient evidence for why their calculations didn't match. She wanted one more opportunity to hear them talk about the lesson and see what they were taking away from the day. She would use this information, along with the data from the exit tickets, to meet with a few select students during the warmup tomorrow. While the majority of the class was completing a bell ringer activity, Mrs. Steinberg would have a few minutes to help students make connections before moving on to the next lesson.

At no time during the lesson did she provide definitions for the terms. In the exit ticket, she asked students to provide a definition of theoretical and experimental probability in their own words. Then she asked them to compare the theoretical probability they calculated to the data they collected for the actual results of their experiment, and explain why they were the same or different. The final question on the exit ticket was: Why might this be important to understand outside of math class?

During the debrief for the CIFT teachers, we reviewed the exit tickets. Not surprisingly, many students used the careers identified during class to state why this might be important to understand outside of class. A few students were able to offer unique examples, and another group left the answer blank. Since the question was intended to assess whether students would be able to see the transfer to application, not if they could brainstorm careers, Mrs. Steinberg told us that she was going to add the question, "What careers rely on probability" to the Broken Record list, then follow up by asking if they would use theoretical, experimental, or both. This would serve as a trigger to prompt the connection.

When introduced to the idea of using Broken Record questioning, most teachers feel a sense of relief. Giving yourself permission to rinse and repeat questions can make lesson planning a bit easier. Most educators offer the same or similar summative assessments for students, typically worded the exact same way. Why, then, would we not include this consistent method of collecting evidence of understanding through the learning process?

Focus and clarity are also supported, which lead to successful learning. We can and probably should pose questions similarly if they are intended to measure the same understanding or prompt the same cognitive thinking. This is not to say they must be identical. Teachers should find a way that is comfortable and authentic to their own instructional style when they ask Broken Record questions.

This Hack supports their learning, too. Maybe more so. Repetition for English learners is an effective way to build language. The Broken Record strategy also helps students see how the same concept can apply in multiple ways or under different conditions. The Broken Record triggers prior knowledge. It also builds a pattern of thinking that students can replicate when the teacher is not near. When students can focus on a few key questions that are most relevant to the purpose of the lesson, they are less likely to get mentally sidetracked.

A lack of consistency in the types of questions teachers pose causes issues of inequity. To be clear, I am not advocating against differentiation, nor am I suggesting a one-question-fits-all perspective. However, I am suggesting that the differentiation is in the task, setting, materials, and even the process to reach the end goal—not the learning goal itself. If it is necessary to take a winding path to the learning target, then take it. Just make sure you do not unintentionally take a different path and end up missing the point of the lesson altogether. Broken Record questions keep you on your path unless you purposefully alter your route.

HACK 6

FILL YOUR BACK POCKET
PREPARE A HANDFUL OF
METACOGNITIVE QUESTIONS

To be prepared is half the victory.
— Miguel de Cervantes Saavedra, Spanish Author

THE PROBLEM: CONTENT QUESTIONS
ALONE ARE NOT ENOUGH

L ESSON PLANNING CENTERS around content learning. Classes are labeled by subject, also known as content areas. State assessments measure student mastery of, you guessed it, content. Even in Hack 5, Broken Record questions are aligned to the learning target. That, too, is content.

The truth is, content is only half of the learning. Yet nearly all the questions revolve around it. It's disproportionate. Content questions do not trigger students to consider how they are interpreting a problem, what strategy they are using to comprehend a complex text, or how they will make choices about the color palette in their paintings. When student questioning falls exclusively in the category of talking about reading, math, or any other content area, we may assume that the students are thinking about thinking.

They aren't. Metacognitive questions, though, are questions that prompt students to do just that: think about *thinking*.

We can access plenty of educational resources about how to craft content questions to take into account both Webb's Depth of Knowledge and Bloom's Taxonomy. But it's not enough for teachers to author the perfect question. It is equally relevant to know how to engage students in actually *thinking* about those five-star questions. If activating student learning is solely dependent upon a sequence of carefully crafted content questions, you will almost certainly find yourself over-scaffolding to support students' abilities to make sense of the questions. Complex content questions without support on how to tackle them through thinking could very well lead to flopped lessons.

How many times have you thought or said to a student, "You are basing that on what you think, not what you learned"? The rhetorical question, "Is that what just happened?" is another example of how we explicitly connect what students are doing to what they are learning. The situation requires great patience when students fall back on their preconceived notions rather than challenging those beliefs with the evidence and experience right in front of them. Limiting your inquiries to content does little to change their approach to thinking.

The Hack is simple: Teach them to think about thinking by using the right sorts of questions.

THE HACK: FILL YOUR BACK POCKET

In order to set yourself up with a balance of content and meta-cognitive questions, fill your back pocket with engagement questions that will help you trigger students to think about thinking. We have more success in creating connections when we deliberately speak to the brain. The beauty of these engagement questions is that you often can keep them in your back pocket and use them in a variety of learning situations. Engagement questions are intended to prompt thinking—which is a part of every content area and does not always have to be content-specific. They trigger students to be mindful of their own thinking, regardless of the topic.

Some engagement questions stand alone and can be used as needed, though I have noticed that teachers tend to favor one or two categories of engagement questions. Using a variety of question types enables students to consider multiple perspectives. Simply stuffing your pocket with a question from different angles will broaden thinking and challenge your learners in new ways. See Image 6.1 for examples of back pocket questions.

Plant engagement questions for later use, too. The Question-Answer Relationship (QAR) strategy developed by Taffy Raphael was originally created to be about comprehension, but lends itself perfectly to asking engagement questions that encourage students to adjust their thinking approach when responding to questions. Raphael offers four types of relationships between a question and an answer. These relationships reflect how a student approaches an answer.

There are two categories within QAR: In the Text and In the Head. Each category has two Question-Answer Relationships, for a total of four combinations.

Back Pocket Questions

	Justification	Aesthetic	
	How do you know? Can you prove it? What is your evidence? Why do you think that? How can you be sure? On what are you basing your answer? Does this always apply?	How do you feel about that? Are you sure? How confident are you in your response? How would you feel if...? What advice would you give? Do you agree with ___? How has your thinking changed? How might someone else respond?	

Experiential

What does this remind you of?

When have you seen this before?

Does this surprise you?

What is this similar to?

How can you relate to this?

Cognitive

What do you think will happen?

What do you estimate?

Why did the author/scientist/ mathematician...?

Is there anything missing?

Are there any other possibilities?

Interpretive

What's the meaning behind...

Is that a good decision?

What is meant by ___?

What does this symbolize?

What is the significance?

Clarification

What is the connotative meaning?

Can you explain that differently?

How would you define that?

Is there another way to say that?

Are you trying to say...

Image 6.1

124

Right There: Answers to questions that can be found in one place in the text.

Think and Search: Answer is found only in the text, but in multiple locations.

Author and Me: Answer comes from the reader's head and what the text says.

On My Own: Answer comes from the reader's head and does not require text.

Sample Text:

Coloring is not just for kindergarten anymore. Bookstores and grocery checkout lanes sell coloring books that even adults can enjoy. Intricate patterns and detailed images provide a canvas for people to splash with all hues of the rainbow. Some doctors are even recommending that patients with anxiety use the black-and-white pages from these books. Adult coloring books are advertised as ways to help reduce stress or just unwind and relax. Some buyers are ordering online and having them delivered right to their homes. Could it be that this childhood activity is more popular with people over eighteen these days?

Question: Where are adult coloring books being sold?

- **Right There Answer:** A grocery store is one place adult coloring books are sold. (The answer is found in the second sentence. The reader could put a finger on it.)

- **Think and Search Answer:** Three places adult coloring books are sold are bookstores, grocery checkout lanes, and online. (The answer is found in the second and sixth sentences in the text. The reader has to look in multiple locations throughout the text to generate this answer.)

- **Author and Me Answer:** Adult coloring books could probably be found on Amazon. (The text supplies the information that buyers are ordering coloring books online. The reader adds schema to the answer by identifying Amazon as a specific online shopping option. The answer combines information from both the text and the reader.)

- **On My Own Answer:** My mom bought an adult coloring book at a dollar store. (The reader does not use information from the text. The answer comes from their own experience.)

These examples illustrate what can happen when a single question is posed. Depending on the cognitive approach the student takes to answer the question, the student can provide a variety of answers that are all correct.

Let's apply this even further. Suppose this sample text is used to teach students about making predictions using textual evidence. A logical question might be: What information might we find in the next paragraph?

Student Response: I predict the next paragraph will be about cutting and pasting, because that's what they do in kindergarten.

A teacher hearing this response will be able to recognize that the student is thinking about their own experience in kindergarten. The justification given does not come from the text, though, and does not show that the student can use textual evidence to prove their prediction. Now what?

Possible Teacher Responses:

- What evidence from the text tells you cutting and pasting will be next? (This disregards the justification the student provided and redirects the student back to the text.)

> **Now when a student says, "I can't find the answer in the book," you can respond with, "That's because it's a Think and Search Question-Answer Relationship." Then send the student back to think and search.**

- What do you know about transitions? (This hints to the student that a transition would give a clue as to what might be coming in the next paragraph. No reference to the reasoning provided by the student.)

- What does the last sentence suggest? (This directs students to where the answer might be, and again, ignores the cognitive process the student actually used.)

- Does the text reference cutting and pasting? (This addresses the student response but does not assist the student with considering a different way to generate a response.)

- You're giving me an On Your Own answer. What would an Author and Me response be? (This labels the student response as a specific type of relationship and redirects the student to reconsider their thinking in a different way without giving any content support.)

Teach students how questions and answers relate to extending their options, and you will redirect their thinking. Now when a student says, "I can't find the answer in the book," you can respond with, "That's because it's a Think and Search Question-Answer Relationship." Then send the student back to think and search.

WHAT YOU CAN DO TOMORROW

- **Expand the variety of your questions.** Using the categories in the solution, determine whether you have questions of a specific type that find their way into your pocket. If so, broaden the kinds of questions you pose. I tend to gravitate to justification questions. They are regularly at the tip of my tongue. Because I recognize that it is less common for me to ask a clarification question, I tuck one away and look for an opportunity to pose it.

- **Attend to verbs.** Use the thinking process you want students to use when you formulate questions. General questions like, "How are you doing?" or "How is it going?" are open-ended, maybe to a fault. You might get replies that relate to how students are feeling, how they're managing time, and what quality of work they are producing. A simple "good" is usually satisfactory for a teacher making quick rounds. Yet it doesn't really give much substance. Switching out the unspecific verb for a verb that inspires the desired thinking process will trigger a more cognitive reply.

How are you doing? → How are you comparing/contrasting?

How is it going? → How is it relating?

- **Be deliberate when using Think Alouds.** A Think Aloud is an instructional strategy that teachers use to model expert thinking. Students often believe that teachers don't have to think about things; they just know them. Use Think Alouds to illustrate a pattern of thinking that students might use when faced with something that stumps them. They should be brief narrations of the thinking that transpires in your head.

Following are simple and powerful traits of the most effective Think Alouds:

    - Use the pronoun "I."

    - Model ways to think through a challenge.

    - Do not include Q&A with the students.

    - Plan in advance based on what is difficult for students.

- Expose struggle and the process of problem-solving.
- Include ideas that you've considered but dismissed, and why you dismissed them.
- Close with an invitation for students to reflect on what they noticed about the teacher's thinking and how that can help them.

- **Follow a content question with another question.** Initially, justification questions are the likely choice for follow-up questions. A student gives a response and you ask how they determined that response. You will know you're establishing the expectation that students expose their reasoning when they offer evidence for their response without being asked. This does not take you off the hook for asking a follow-up question. When they provide justification, questions that question their thinking come into play:

  - Would anyone else have a different perspective?
  - Was that the first thing you considered?
  - What are some possible exceptions to your idea?
  - How might others critique your thought?

A BLUEPRINT FOR FULL IMPLEMENTATION

Step 1: Introduce QAR with In the Text and In the Head categories.

The first step to putting Question-Answer Relationships in your back pocket is to teach students the two places answers are generated: In the Text and In the Head. The most challenging concept for students when learning about Question-Answer Relationships is to have a clear picture of where the information comes from.

The first thought might be to teach the four QARs one at a time. That's step two. First, introduce the two categories of answers that come exclusively from the text, and answers that come from the students' heads. Doing so before acquainting students with examples within the categories helps them figure out how to process a question and correlate a response more effectively.

Step 2: Generate questions and answers for each QAR.

Once students can demonstrate an understanding of questions that have to be answered from the text, versus questions that are answered in their heads, present the types of QARs to them. Sequence the reveal in this order:

First, define Right There and Think and Search QARs under the category of In the Text. In this step, it is important to clarify that Think and Search might require thinking in your head, but doesn't collect additional information beyond what is in the text. For example, a Think and Search might be: "How can this text be summarized? What is the main idea?" Just because the answer is not explicit does not mean it is an In Your Head response. Summarizing a text or identifying a theme do not add information from the students' schema. But they do require thinking, and thinking about the text. Spend time providing various examples of questions and answers together. Students can determine whether they can find the relationship between them in one or multiple places in the text.

Next, share Author and Me and On My Own QARs. You might choose to begin with On My Own, then move to Author and Me. As with the In the Text QARs, provide students with combinations of questions and answers, and have them sort within this category. Before bringing all four QARs into the mix, gather formative data so that students can bucket On My Own and Author and Me QARs consistently.

CAUTION: THIS IS ABOUT THE RELATIONSHIP BETWEEN QUESTIONS AND ANSWERS, NOT ABOUT SORTING TYPES OF QUESTIONS. STUDENTS NEED BOTH PIECES OF INFORMATION TO DETERMINE THE RELATIONSHIP.

When you bring all four QARs into the mix, you can anticipate that if there is a struggle to sort the QARs, it is likely a struggle to decipher between Author and Me and Think and Search. Plan a Think Aloud to allow students to hear how you would think through distinguishing one from the other.

Provide students with short texts along with questions and correlating answers. Task them with determining the type of QAR, and providing their reasoning. Gradually increase the length of the text. Continue to provide both a question and an answer. Offer all four types of QARs, and use the Broken Record question, "Why is it this QAR and not another?" Since there are only four QARs, the students have a pretty good shot at a correct guess. Listen for the music of their justification, and don't be satisfied with just an accurate label. You are almost ready to put those QAR questions in your pocket.

Step 3: Have students generate answers.

As students master the categorization of QARs, move to providing only questions. Have students generate their answers, then determine what type of QAR they used for their responses. To encourage pinball talk, assign students to work in collaborative groups of four students each. Print cards with each type of QAR listed on them, and pass them out to each student in the group. Using four different pieces of text (or breaking a longer text into four sections), give students four questions per section for a total of sixteen questions. Design the questions so they lend themselves to each type of QAR.

Task students with collectively answering each question. Then, one by one, have each student say whether the QAR matches their card, and why or why not. In round two, ask them to rotate cards and follow the same protocol. After four rotations, each student will have identified all the QARs and responded to the Broken Record question twelve times. Before moving on to step four, gather formative data to be sure students are proficient in step three.

Step 4: Have students generate questions.

The next level of implementation is for students to analyze the QAR from the question angle. Assign students, still in their groups, to craft one question for each type of QAR based on a piece of text. Review their questions to check that they can represent all four QARs. Tell students to give their questions to another group. The second group determines answers and labels the QAR between the first group's question and their answer. Of course, they should provide justification for their decisions. You may repeat this process by having groups switch with another group. Provide feedback about their justification of the QAR.

To verify that every student has mastered the Question-Answer Relationship, repeat this step with individual students rather than collaborative groups. As students were first applying their new learning, the support of their peers and the opportunity to have dialogue will deepen their understanding, provide multiple opportunities for practice, and build efficacy.

Step 5: Use the language of QAR to adjust student responses.

After steps one through four, you can reap the benefit of planting questions. Evoke a different approach to analyzing a question by pulling a relationship out of your pocket. Schools that systematically teach students QAR leverage its impact across grade levels and content areas.

Once students understand how questions and answers can relate to one another, the reference to using Right There or Think and Search questions can be applied to both reading and experiences. Science experiments, for example, present opportunities to redirect students. Use evidence from their observations, along with their own background knowledge. When you pull an Author and Me question out of your pocket, modify it by using "the experiment and me" instead. It indicates to students that their investigation requires that they apply their prior learning in order to make sense out of what they are discovering.

There are no holes in your pocket, either. Stuff these questions back in for safekeeping. Whenever your students need a cognitive prompt to approach a question differently, your questions will be ready.

OVERCOMING PUSHBACK

Knowing how questions and answers relate doesn't deepen content knowledge. The intent for teaching students QAR is to assist them in being mindful about how they think about the content. Acknowledge to students that they are not going to be able to put their finger on a Think and Search question to extend their perseverance. But this will affect the approaches they take, which will increase their understanding.

It feels contrived when I plan questions in advance. Forethought in questions, both for content and for engagement, is less about creating a script and more about being intentional. Put thought into how to frame a question where students might struggle and need support, and you will be a little more prepared when those situations arise. Arming yourself with a handful of questions smooths the lesson and presents your message more clearly.

What if I ask the wrong kind of question? Then you do. It is not going to ruin the lesson or prevent students from learning. Centering your attention on how and when, and what questions to deliver, will sharpen your questioning skills. Pay attention to patterns in the way you pose questions and be alert to how students react to them. When you find a winner, put it in your back pocket for a bit. See what kind of wear you get out of it.

THE HACK IN ACTION

One of my visits to Ms. Annette Buttle's elementary classroom highlighted how she differentiated QAR for her second-grade readers. Like in most of the classrooms in Soledad USD in California, the majority of her students were English learners. Not only were they learning to read, but they were also learning to read in a language that was spoken in only a few of their homes. Providing them with vocabulary to talk about how their questions and answers connected was time well-spent when it came to pushing their learning to move from Right There to Think and Search questions throughout the year.

Ms. Buttle planned a progression of a few questions, knowing she would be posing many more as the lesson unfolded. Her students had experience identifying characters and setting in the text. She wanted to prepare them to piece together information from multiple parts of the text. Surprisingly, Ms. Buttle was not familiar with the Question-Answer Relationship strategy yet. But she was clearly talking about Think and Search questions without even knowing it.

Characters were brought into the story at various points, and students noted wherever a character was introduced using highlighter tape to keep track. Ms. Buttle stacked her questions in a clever way to ease students into the notion of using more than one location within the text to find an answer. She asked her learners the overarching question: What characters are in this story? After they named each character, she replayed the Broken Record question: Does the story have any other characters? She followed that with a request for evidence in the text: How do you know who the characters are?

The students added tape on multiple pages within their books, and one page even had two characters highlighted. In each phase of the lesson, Ms. Buttle used a combination of Broken Record and In Your Pocket questions to create a balanced learning experience for students. She focused on what they were learning, then used metacognitive questions to highlight a transferable skill.

To differentiate the lesson, she had some students highlight every time a character was referenced, while others only highlighted the first time a character was introduced. After the students were done highlighting, the students who flagged every time a character was mentioned turned back to the beginning of the story. These students flipped through page by page until they found a piece of highlighter tape. They listed the character under the tape on a separate sheet of paper. When they wrote down the name, they removed the tape. If a character who was already on the list was found in the text again, the student made a check mark next to the name on the list and proceeded to remove the highlighter tape.

This added step was intentionally planned for these students because Ms. Buttle predicted that they would find it challenging to use multiple parts of the text to answer questions. She chose to provide them with a strategy that assisted them in being successful. Much like using repeated addition to represent multiplication, Ms. Buttle used repeated Right There QARs to represent a Think and Search with her next question: How many characters are in the story?

Students who only highlighted a character when they were first introduced were able to go back through the text and count their highlights. The other group of students simply counted the characters on their list. Both groups were able to experience the task of finding and applying information throughout the text, but in a guided way that set them up for success without much assistance.

From this experience, she introduced the idea that some questions are in the text, and it requires a system and a lot of searching to answer them. Now Ms. Buttle's students were ready to take on the challenge of more Think and Search questions.

Being prepared does require a play-by-play script that has little room for deviation. One could argue that being prepared is more about knowing what to do when one needs to revise the script. I recall a time or two in my career when I had to communicate information of which I had a limited understanding. I remember thinking, *I hope nobody asks me any questions because this is all I know.* You have to be ready for curve balls to come your way!

A common metaphor used in education, especially in professional learning sessions, is to have more tools in the toolbox. These strategies and tricks of the trade are ready and waiting for you to pull them out when the time comes. The more tools we have, the better prepared we feel. Most of us have plenty of tools related to content. We share mnemonics, acronyms, and silly sayings to help students remember and make sense of content information.

Arming yourself with a variety of question types broadens the perspective you can offer students when thinking about their learning. Justification questions like, "What evidence do you have?" trigger a completely different thought process than aesthetic questions such as, "How has your thinking changed"? Know what angle you want students to explore when reflecting on their learning. Begin with a single question in the right category. For example, if students need to be more thorough in their work, content questions might not be the most effective. A question that draws attention to detail will put them on the right path.

Think of a student who surprised you on an assessment. You expected them to produce better work and concluded that they were rushing through it and didn't put forth their best effort. "Is there anything missing?" which is a cognitive question, will be more productive for the student than a question that revisits details from the lesson.

Students make connections between the what and the how to guide their inquiry. Intentionally revealing the relationships between questions and answers by teaching QAR as a method for processing questions, and defining the four combinations, brings the language into your class's academic vocabulary. Doing so expands your toolbox to include questions that label thinking approaches before initiating the actual thoughts.

HACK 7

MAKE YOURSELF INVISIBLE
ESTABLISH STUDENT-CENTERED PROTOCOLS

It takes real planning to organize this kind of chaos.
— MEL ODOM, SCIENCE FICTION AUTHOR

THE PROBLEM: TEACHERS INCLUDE THEMSELVES IN STUDENT LEARNING

I**F STUDENTS ARE** capable learners, we should get out of their way. But it's not as easy as it sounds for teachers to step aside and allow students to take that cognitive baton and run with it. Teachers always seem to find reasons to think they should include themselves in student learning—even if they shouldn't. When teachers are too visible during learning, *they* own the learning and students become overly dependent on them. Our goal is never to develop dependent learners. We need to provide circumstances and learning structures where students can experience the joy of learning—without their teacher leading them.

I have heard countless teachers admit they have difficulty giving up control of the classroom. When it's a priority to maintain order and structure, whole-class instruction followed by independent practice is an easy pick for lesson design. However, it is not the most effective way to ensure that students get a firm grip on your content. You are holding the cognitive baton during whole-class direct instruction, then sending them off to regurgitate what you said. If the context is more complex, this structure of whole-class to independent learning forces kids to make sense of it on their own.

This sudden jolt from "I do" to "you do alone" is not a gradual release.

Moving to independent practice or individual learning too quickly pretty much guarantees that the students will struggle. When the expectation is that students work individually, their only option to make sense of confusing ideas is to call the teacher over and lessen their struggle. Doing so transfers some of the ownership back to the teacher.

It is possible, even likely, that students could persevere through the struggle with a support system that falls between doing it completely on their own and calling the teacher over for help. That middle ground is student collaboration. If student collaboration is not even offered as an option, though, teachers become the learning partners for twenty-five different students in the classroom. Now who is the hardest worker in the room?

Think of professional development sessions you have attended where the presenter talked and talked. When new learning inspires you, if you are like most teachers, you will want to talk to your fellow department or grade-level teachers and pose your own application questions. What do you think? How could we make this work? In what way does it fit/conflict with our current beliefs and structures? It's a gift to have time to process and plan a way to actually use the information presented to you. If that gift is not provided, most teachers beg their administrators for more time. Why? Because collaboration is a natural part of the learning process. It triggers productive questions that lead to understanding and use of new information. Did you need time alone and a direct line to your principal? Probably not. Conversations with other learners making their own connections are enough support to allow you to get the clarity you need to apply your new learning in meaningful ways.

Students are no different. Bouncing ideas and connections off other learners is an effective way to build a deep understanding of the topic.

Lack of opportunity for those collaborative conversations is an obvious problem. A more nuanced, but legitimate, reason that students do not own their learning to the max is that teachers love to teach. Teachers may almost feel guilty when they don't perceive themselves as "teaching." But this is a belief that conflicts with what these same teachers will often say is their goal: to create learners. Teaching is not the center of learning. Exemplary teaching *activates* learning, but does not necessarily lead it all the time.

As we attempt to provide opportunities for students to talk, we may feel that we aren't doing our jobs. This perception is heightened when an administrator walks into the room. Our students are working productively. The lesson we wrote is going as expected. Yet we feel an overwhelming responsibility to lead the learning. I mean, I am the teacher, right? Shouldn't I be teaching?

Twitter chats and YouTube videos of teachers describing the success of empowering students to own their learning have increased the number of teachers bringing more student talk into their lessons. Still, it's a tall order to set students loose with the expectation that they will figure out both a process for learning and the actual learning of the content simultaneously. The opportunity increases for a bombed lesson. Teachers establish the result—a belief that students are not capable of academic discourse—and revert back to more traditional methods of instruction.

There must be a method to the madness, or you just have classroom chaos.

But if we want our students to truly get into the subject and learn, and if we want them to think about thinking and build the connections for doing it again and again, we need to find a way to get out of *their* way. We need to make ourselves invisible.

THE HACK: MAKE YOURSELF INVISIBLE

Do not lose sight of the fact that learning does not require a teacher to do the teaching. The very best lessons I have observed provide the conditions for students to be their own teachers. The only way to accomplish this utopian classroom is to make yourself invisible and step aside so students can own their learning and support the learning of their peers.

The best way to do this is to implement student-centered protocols.

Students deepen their knowledge around skills and concepts by using discourse to make sense of information. Natural questioning and thinking occur through conversation, and it helps them move toward clarity. The deeper their understanding, the more likely they are to use their knowledge in relevant and unfamiliar situations. This is the ultimate goal of learning. It sounds so easy. But creating successful collaborative learning structures in the classroom—and then getting out of the way—requires planning, practice, and patience.

In other words, there must be a method to the madness, or you just have classroom chaos.

There is no shortage of structures and protocols to set up opportunities for students to engage in thinking with their peers. As they wrestle with difficult or complex ideas, they build perseverance and efficacy, and those traits will help them both in your class and in the future. The systems you choose should give them a guideline for thinking about what they need to do—without you doing it for them. Essentially, providing the conditions for learning in an organized way means you can make yourself invisible. Following are a few protocols that foster interdependence and are designed to embed accountability for all group members.

Full Jigsaw: A properly executed jigsaw has three parts. Each has a distinct and important purpose in the collaborative learning phase. Shortcuts in facilitating a jigsaw reduce its effectiveness, so to leverage the greatest benefit, do not skip steps.

If comprehending a text means following a sequence that builds throughout the text, then it does not make sense to assign one student to read step four before steps one through three. Jigsaws are best when a text is structured categorically. Breaking pieces of the task up should create complete understandings that can be summarized independently. Each of these small summaries is then puzzled back together to reveal the complete picture.

Part One: Expert Groups. Determine the number of components for the learning. Assign each student one of the pieces to study. Group students who are studying the same parts together, and provide them with enough time to make sense of their assigned parts and become experts. Provide graphic organizers and summary sheets to these expert groups to support them in taking notes and comprehending their pieces of the puzzle. They serve as resources for students to use in Part Two of the jigsaw.

> TIP: WHEN ASSIGNING EXPERT AND TEACHING GROUPS, CONSIDER STUDENTS WHO WOULD BENEFIT FROM HAVING A PARTNER. ENGLISH LEARNERS OR THOSE WHO HAVE DIFFICULTY BECOMING AN EXPERT MIGHT TEACH AS A DUO WITH SOMEONE ELSE IN THE EXPERT GROUP.

It is important that every member of the expert group is capable of speaking to their topic. Do not cut this time short or rush through this step. One unprepared expert will result in confusion in your classroom. This phase is a logical spot for a formative assessment to help you confirm that everyone is prepared to move on.

Part Two: Teaching Groups. Students reshuffle into new groups with one person from each expert group in a teaching group. The groups are tasked with taking the content they discussed and learned about in their expert group, and sharing it with their teaching group. They may use their notes. Students who are learners in the teaching group are encouraged to take notes. One by one, the students share their pieces of the

> IF GROUPS DO NOT FINISH AT THE SAME TIME, DROP REFLECTING QUESTIONS ON THE TABLES TO KEEP THEM ENGAGED IN DIALOGUE.

puzzle and jigsaw all of the content together. The goal here is for each member to be exposed and learn the component parts, and begin seeing connections to the big picture.

Part Three: Big Picture Groups. Send students back to their expert groups. These are the groups that initially only looked at one part of the whole picture. Each expert came from a different teaching group, and together, they can use their notes and reference the dialogue from their teaching groups to see the big picture. This third step reveals any gaps created in the teaching groups, and by design offers multiple opportunities for students to fill their gaps collaboratively with other learners.

TIP: DO ANY SYNTHESIZING IN THIS GROUP. IT KEEPS THE COGNITIVE DEMAND HIGH. ALL OF THE LEARNERS ARE IN THE SAME BOAT WHEN IT COMES TO THE PORTIONS OF THE CONTENT ON WHICH THEY DID NOT BECOME EXPERTS.

Round Table Discussion: In this protocol, students work together to include input from each member of the group. Use a simple template to assist with keeping track of everyone's contributions. This structure is helpful when learning about points of view, summarizing and synthesizing, and many other complex thinking formats.

Chalk Talk: This is a silent "talk" where the writing utensils do all of the communicating. It can be used for brainstorming, summarizing, or deepening learning. The teacher prepares a question or topic for students to think about and the students write it in the center of a large piece of paper. Assign groups large enough to build on one another's thoughts, and small enough for everyone to have access to the paper at the same time. Three to five is a good number to try first. Give each group member a different color marker. Before starting the chalk talk, the students write their names on the chart paper using their markers. This provides a key for them and you to track the thoughts of each student.

Set a timer and launch students into sharing their thinking, without talking, on the chart paper. They can connect and comment on their classmates' contributions—but in writing.

One of the benefits of this routine is that it gives quieter students a voice, and learners who require a little extra think time are not put on the spot to think too quickly. Because the other students are busy reading and writing on the paper, it is less noticeable if one of the students begins writing after everyone else.

Change up this protocol by changing the number of questions or topics you provide. Each group can respond to the same question, or you can rotate them through stations and give them the opportunity to think about multiple questions or topics. Alter this protocol to fit your purposes and time allowances.

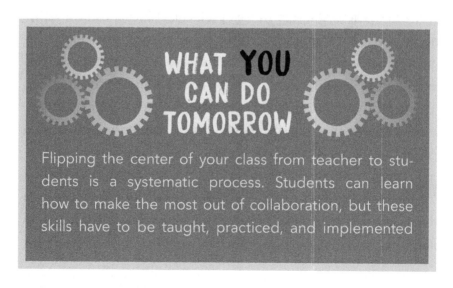

WHAT YOU CAN DO TOMORROW

Flipping the center of your class from teacher to students is a systematic process. Students can learn how to make the most out of collaboration, but these skills have to be taught, practiced, and implemented successfully. Here are a few ways to get students ready for highly structured protocols, or practice the skills throughout the week:

- **Pause after ten minutes or less for a Partner Share.** You can feel it. Students are getting antsy. You're losing their focus. This is a great time to pull out a quick Turn and Talk. Students can process, paraphrase, connect, and predict. The amount of time you spend redirecting students who are disconnecting is much better spent with a thirty- to ninety-second Partner Share.

- **Hack the Turn and Talk.** Ramp up your Turn and Talk while practicing speaking and listening skills by making it a Turn and *Ask*. Prompt Student A to pose a question to Student B. You can even give Student A the question. The idea in the early stages of building a back-and-forth dialogue is less about crafting the question and more about creating an actual conversation. This strategy can create another unintended benefit for your quieter students if you prompt students to pick who will go first. Chances are, your more talkative students will volunteer. Give the first speaker a question to pose. Now you're inviting the student who typically gets shut out to be the first one to respond to the question.

- **Be mindful of your eye contact.** If you are roaming the room to monitor students working together, position yourself so you are close enough to hear their conversation, but do not include yourself in it. When you make eye contact with the student speaking, their natural tendency will be to shift the conversation away from peers and turn it to a student-teacher dialogue. Although this might not be your intent, some students feel obligated to share their thoughts with the teacher. They might be looking for affirmation that they are on the right track or showing off how much they have already learned. Either way, they do not need you at this point, so there is no reason to engage in dialogue with them. Be invisible.

- **Model effective collaboration skills.** If you find that a group is being unproductive, instead of intervening as a teacher, temporarily join their group and perform as a peer. Take a seat and offer talk moves that can help them use one another to prevent their progress from stalling. This might mean you model questions that solicit voices from quieter team members. "Travis, we haven't heard your thoughts yet. What is your perspective?" When Travis responds, look at other group members so Travis doesn't begin having a dialogue with just you. Travis will likely try to respond to you first, but as mentioned in the previous bullet, if you refuse to make eye contact, he will move on to someone else who he can engage. Now you can slip out of the group and allow them to carry on their conversation. The support you provide might not be about content, but about helping them access one another and build collaboration skills.

Here are common questions that can support collaboration:

- What other ideas or perspectives might there be?
- There seem to be many thoughts on the table. How can they be narrowed?
- There don't seem to be many thoughts on the table. What is missing?
- Remember, the purpose is for everyone to learn (insert learning target here). How are you ensuring that everyone has the same level of understanding?
- What goals did you set for your team? How will you meet those goals?

- **Monitor with a clipboard.** One of the biggest challenges for teachers during student collaboration is resisting the urge to butt in. Carrying a clipboard with a list of student names and key concepts or collaboration skills you're expecting helps you observe without feeling the need to interject. As you float through the class, notice academic vocabulary, patterns in discourse, and how students are communicating. If you are practicing a protocol, make sure students are following the steps and their roles effectively. Even if you are launching a basic Turn and Ask, listen for evidence that students are able to discuss the idea thoroughly.

Just because you cannot get to all of your students doesn't mean there is not a benefit to listening in on a few. Move away from your spot at the front of the class and get students comfortable with you being close to them—even if you are not interacting with them. This is one way to begin your invisibility. If students see that you have your own task, they will be less likely to pull you into their conversation simply because you are close.

- **Use sounds to signal routine transitions.** In your daily activities, pull back from verbally cueing students to follow the routine. Instead of saying, "It's time to clean up," use a sound. Music, chimes, claps, or a bell can all serve as a signal to students to initiate a routine for putting their supplies away and preparing for the next transition. Replacing your voice with an alternate notification will reduce the amount of talking you are doing. Now you can reserve your words for instruction. The more you talk, the more opportunities for them to tune you out. Make your words count by saving them for the most valuable times. Find ways to use sound for other purposes. Bringing students' attention to the whole group and rotating learning stations are other examples of when you might take advantage of this strategy. If you prefer to use a silent signal like flickering the lights or raising your hand in the air, that works too.

A BLUEPRINT FOR FULL IMPLEMENTATION

Step 1: Establish a system for grouping students.

How you group students for collaborative learning is the first step in disappearing from the center of the lesson. But this can feel like a complex and overwhelming task—and it can take a lot of time and energy to figure out how to do it. You must take into account so many variables. Friendships, skill levels, personalities, work ethics, and interests are all factors many teachers throw into the mixing pot when assigning groups.

It will tighten your protocol and permit you to be invisible if you create a system you can access at any point throughout the

TIP: WHEN A FEW STUDENTS NEED YOUR SUPPORT, DON'T DIVIDE THEM INTO GROUPS IN HOPES THAT THEIR PEERS WILL FILL IN THE GAPS. THIS REQUIRES YOU TO SUPPORT EVERY GROUP. MAKE YOURSELF INVISIBLE WITH THE MAJORITY OF STUDENTS, EVEN IF THAT MEANS BEING VISIBLE TO THOSE WHO NEED SUPPORT.

school year. Clock Partners, as shared in Hack 1, are one example of how you can connect students with partners based on different criteria. Another option is to use symbols with multiple attributes and secure them randomly to students' desks. You might have numbers inside shapes printed on colored paper. Now you have three ways to group students. Gather all the ones, twos, and threes together. Next time you might select to have the triangles, squares, and circles working together. Then they might quickly check in with another orange, blue, or green partner.

This strategy is particularly popular in secondary classrooms, when students come and go throughout the day. With a multi-layered system for grouping students, you can sort students into teams with a simple statement. Assigning seven groups by calling off all twenty-eight names in chunks of four will keep you at the center of attention for far longer than, "Find your shape group and assign the blue shape to begin."

The sooner you can activate your invisibility, the better. This first decision is a doozy. How students are grouped can make or break the entire lesson.

Step 2: Select a handful of various protocols to use all year.

Always ask yourself about the intention for your groups. The underlying factor should include how you remain invisible for the protocol. If you plan to differentiate, you will want to put students together who will benefit from the changes you made to the content, process, product, or learning environment. To increase risk-taking, give students some choice so they are comfortable with their groups. For example, pair students up with their elbow partners, then allow the two of them to choose another pair to launch a Think-Pair-Square with the four of them. To bring in different perspectives, try more heterogeneous groupings.

Whatever protocol you decide on, take the time to consider your role and how you will resist doing cognitive work the students could do for themselves. If you do not have a plan to keep yourself invisible, you might find yourself in the middle of the group's discussion without a true need to be there.

Step 3: Teach protocols independent from content.

The benefit of teaching protocols is that it saves you time down the road. Just like teaching students a morning routine frees up time for housekeeping tasks like attendance and checking in with absent students, learning routines provide more classroom minutes to focus on content. The familiarity with the routine helps with your invisibility. Stopping to remind students of the next steps every few minutes brings attention to you.

As students are learning a new routine or talk protocol, separate the procedural learning from the academic learning. Give them simple and fun topics to discuss as they get acclimated to the process of collaborative thinking. For example, if students are learning how to ask relevant questions, focus solely on the characteristics of those questions. Ask students to talk about their first memory or describe their favorite relative. Choose a topic for which students are not likely to have a frame of reference. That way, they cannot rely on their own experiences, but will have to execute their listening skills in order to successfully ask relevant questions.

Don't complicate the task by asking them to discuss a piece of complex text right away. When learners are forced to split their attention between learning a new procedure and learning new content, they are not likely to master both. Scaffold for them by isolating the process so they will become comfortable with the protocol. Once they know it, you can use it to process academic content. You will more easily disappear and allow students to rely on the protocol if you let them get comfortable with it first.

Step 4: Practice the protocols.

Remind students that the protocol is designed to walk them through a sequence of learning so they can work together as a team. Your role is to observe and notice. They should rely on one another for help, not you. As students are introduced to a new protocol, continue to use it throughout the day or week. The idea of establishing a learning routine is to make it second nature so it can then be used to process more complex kinds of prompts related to learning.

Pay attention to your invisibility. Do you need to clarify the steps of the routine? Do students have all the materials they need? Is the timing appropriate for them to complete the learning task? Repeating the routine allows your students to get more comfortable with speaking and listening to one another more instead of calling you over.

As you practice, call students' attention to how productive they are being in their groups, and how they are starting to rely less on you. Your efforts to make yourself invisible should not be a secret. Invite students to share the goal of persevering through the task and using the protocol to help them work through any confusion they might face. You can begin to transition from teaching the routine with familiar topics, to using the familiar routine with topics you're teaching. The lessons will maintain a sense of security that can keep students relaxed, and you can return to being invisible.

Step 5: Reflect and adapt protocols based on student feedback.

Establishing protocols can take multiple rehearsals. Between each practice, take the time to prompt students to consider the effectiveness of the routine. Possible questions for reflection include:

- What are the benefits of this protocol?

- What are the disadvantages of this protocol?

- How could this protocol be improved to support everyone's learning?

- Would this be effective in another lesson?

- What was the least-effective part of this protocol? How do you know?

- What could be done to improve this protocol in the future?

- What else should we keep in mind for the next time this protocol is used?

- What allowed your group to work together?

- How did your group respond when you thought you needed help from the teacher?

- If you asked for assistance, did you really need it? Why/why not?

Take student feedback and apply it to make modifications to the protocol, then repeat the reflection to determine if the modifications did indeed improve the opportunity for learning, or if different tweaks would be more helpful.

OVERCOMING PUSHBACK

It is tempting to abandon more student-centered activities when they do not go perfectly. It's also difficult to let go of control. Some teachers might even try to rationalize why it just won't work in their classrooms. Being invisible is not as straightforward as it sounds. Don't give up; it might just take patience.

Some groups finish early and have nothing to do. Preparing one or two follow-up questions or alternate applications can help early completers remain on task. For example, if groups are solving a math problem, a follow-up might be to ask a group to write a similar problem and outline how they would expect another team to solve it. If students are analyzing a piece of literature, challenge them to consider events in the story from a different perspective.

Another option for keeping learning groups productive is to ask students to evaluate the effectiveness of their team. What collaborative skills did they execute well, and what goals might they set for their team in the future?

Extending time in groups is only necessary if the activity they are tasked with is chronological or has a specified completion point. If students are brainstorming, do not feel obligated to give all teams enough time to exhaust all of their ideas. It's beneficial to pause their work when engagement is still high. That way, you can leverage the momentum into the next part of the lesson.

One student will do all the work while the others sit back and let them. Collaborative learning is more than just putting students in groups and asking them to complete a task collectively. The purpose of collaborative learning is two-fold. First, it reinforces speaking and listening skills they will need to communicate effectively with others (see Hack 4: Be a Pinball Wizard). Second, it helps individuals solidify their understanding so they can be independently successful. The goal is always for each student to learn. The way to decrease the circumstance where one student takes the lead is to establish accountability throughout.

I am not suggesting superficial jobs like "materials manager" or "timekeeper." These roles might be necessary for a group to get prepared and stay productive. However, they do not require any active thinking and therefore do not meet the criteria for holding students accountable for engaged learning. The first of two main approaches to holding individual students accountable is to design the protocol so it requires each member of the team to hold a piece of learning that the entire group needs in order to accomplish their collective goal. The full jigsaw, round table discussion, and reciprocal teaching are examples of structures that fit this format.

The second accountability method is to allow students to process information in their groups, but work independently to use that learning in their own ways. Give One, Get One is a protocol that helps students use their peers to gather information, then use it to make meaning on their own.

I am the teacher; I am supposed to be helping them. Don't confuse helping them with doing it for them. The goal is for students to learn, not for a teacher to be a rock star educator. The greatest way a teacher can *help* a student is to provide that student with the skills to acquire knowledge. That's the whole point of making yourself invisible. Breaking through struggle and accomplishing success is more beneficial for learners than merely completing a task. Ask yourself if you're helping them learn or helping them finish the assignment.

When I am supporting one group, there is always another group that needs me. Teachers foster this familiar scene of running around the classroom putting out fires from group to group, for a few reasons:

- Students are uncomfortable with struggle, and so is the teacher. In order for students to bust through a challenge, they have to wrestle with it. The longer we can extend the time students are willing to stick with a problem, the more stamina and perseverance they build. This requires the teacher to recognize when the efforts students are making are moving them forward, or have the potential to make progress. Then let that journey take its course.

- Teachers make themselves too accessible to students. I am not suggesting you are literally invisible, but there is no need to hover over students and wait for them to ask you a question. Or worse, approach a group and explicitly ask, "Do you have any questions?" If they have questions, they should grapple with them first before calling you over.

Students say they learn better when they listen to me. It shouldn't surprise us that some students would be more comfortable watching the teacher do all the work. Don't fall for it. There is merit to direct instruction in short spurts when it comes to building surface-level knowledge. On the flip side, you cannot open a child's mind and pour your deep understanding into it. Students have to grow their own dendrites, and that happens when they think—not just listen.

THE HACK IN ACTION

One New York classroom I observed used a gallery walk to help the teacher disappear. Middle school social studies teacher Mr. Dean Bourazeris designed a lesson so students could explore the guiding question: How interconnected was the world before the age of exploration? Before class, he posted maps around the room to create stations. Each map included lines that represented trade routes. Mr. Bourazeris planned a gallery walk using a See-Think-Wonder protocol. He modeled the See-Think-Wonder with the entire class. In the prebrief, he shared that he was not sure students would know what *interconnected* was. He was prepared to signal them to separate the "inter" from "connected" to help them access and apply the prefix and root word skills they learned in ELA.

The class was sorted into five groups, one for each map. Each student had a clipboard and a note-taking sheet to document what they noticed from the map, what conclusions they drew from those observations, and what inquiries they generated. A visual timer with a bell indicated when their time at the current map was over, and initiated the movement to the next map. He planned five minutes at five maps. For twenty-five consecutive minutes, the entire class of seventh-graders was interpreting maps and building on one another's observations. Rotations from map to map took literally two seconds. No instructional time was wasted. They collaboratively drew conclusions about what they were noticing.

What was Mr. Bourazeris doing? Observing, listening, and taking notes. He was clearly enjoying it. There was a relaxed feel in the room, and students were engaged. Their noticings and wonderings about the maps deepened their conversations. Mr. Bourazeris silently witnessed students asking genuine and relevant questions within their groups, then collaboratively attempting to find evidence in the maps that could lead them to clarity. As he traveled the perimeter of the room, students barely noticed his approach. They hardly saw him there. He would occasionally drop a question on the group for them to ponder, then swiftly slipped far enough away that he was not easily accessible. He turned his body so he was facing another direction, but his ear remained on the group to eavesdrop on how they processed his query.

Mr. Bourazeris's superpower? Invisibility.

It might sound easy-peasy to hand the reins over to students and let them do all the work. However, it requires careful and deliberate planning to pull it off well. Using student-centered protocols is not less work for the teacher. It is *different* work. Most of it transpires in the planning process. Careful thought produces lessons that appear to run themselves. When details are intentionally considered, the actual class time frees the teacher's mind to focus on noticing how and what students are learning. Students build independence and confidence.

Here are considerations when planning your invisibility:

- What norms do I need to establish? What criteria should I use to group students?

- What do I need in a protocol?

- How can I minimize wasted time?

- What room arrangement will work best for this protocol?

- What resources do we need?

- Will the group produce a single product, or will each student have their own?

- What kind of feedback do I want to collect after the protocol is completed?

- What will I be doing when students are working?

- How will materials be managed?

- How will the protocol be introduced?

- Are there any modifications that would improve the protocol for my students?

- What else am I missing?

HACK 8

HEAR THE MUSIC
LISTEN FOR CORRECT THINKING,
NOT JUST CORRECT ANSWERS

I frequently hear music in the very heart of noise.
— George Gershwin, Composer

THE PROBLEM: TEACHERS ASSUME A CORRECT
ANSWER MEANS THE STUDENT "GOT IT"

MANY TEACHERS USE questions to check for student understanding of concepts and learning, then use correct responses as evidence that the students "got it." The trouble with using answers to determine mastery is that answers are not transferable. Logical thinking and reasoning are transferable. When we expect that a right answer today is an indication of right answers for life, we find ourselves baffled when students are not able to repeat their thinking the very next day.

Hearing a right answer from a student frequently causes teachers to assume that students used a sound thinking process to reach that answer. But they rarely validate that assumption. If we don't ask students to *justify* their answers, it's like watching a music video on mute. We ignore the best part: the lullaby of logical reasoning. Sometimes students guess. Sometimes they memorize answers. Sometimes they are led to the right response through a line of well-intended spoon-feeding (see Hack 9: Scaffold, Don't Spoon-Feed).

Our reaction to incorrect answers is equally important. Answer-seeking teachers might hear a wrong answer and say, "That's not exactly what I was looking for" or "Hmm … who can help Jeremiah with this question?" This is a missed opportunity to reveal, address, and redirect misconceptions before students develop them into truths.

This action also communicates to the student that his learning is not the priority, but announcing the right answer is the priority. If another student knows the right answer, it gives the teacher a sense that the students learned, and that it is okay to move on with the lesson. The assumption is that the student who didn't know the answer will suddenly understand, simply through hearing the right answer from a peer. It is likely that this peer already knew the answer, though, so the result is that neither student experiences new learning.

Teachers foster fixed mindsets when they only welcome and celebrate right answers. The solution is simple: Answer-seeking perspective needs a change of tune.

THE HACK: HEAR THE MUSIC

We can almost hear the sound of a choir joining in a collective "ahhhh" when a student declares an answer and it is right.

Alternately, virtual alarms sound off in an experienced teacher's head when a string of erroneous answers pour out of a child's mouth. But we need to listen to what lies beyond the answers. Mute the choir or alarms until you hear the music behind how the student reached those answers. Take the additional step and ask the student to expose his thought process. This allows you to make sure he has a solid path of logic that he can replicate in different settings. It also provides students with the opportunity to be metacognitive about their learning. How did I get to this answer? Does my thinking make sense? Are there any exceptions to my assumptions? Am I certain, or do I still have some wonderings?

In order to get inside a student's head, use justification questions. Use them when the student's answer is correct ... *and* when the answer is clearly not correct. Maintain a poker face when requesting justification, or students will use the social cues to influence how they articulate their thinking. Test this theory by asking a question typically reserved for wrong answers: "Are you sure?" When a student gives a right answer, watch how the student responds to "Are you sure?" It is a closed-ended, yes/no question that rarely solicits a yes/no answer. Even the youngest learners understand that this question is adult code for "Your answer is wrong."

Rather than triggering a mind frame of confusion and guessing, pose a question like, "How did you reach that response?" Their answers might surprise you. They may be over-generalizing old learning, or straight-out guessing.

For example, when learning about states of matter, Gabrielle shows her understanding from previous lessons by announcing, "Molecules in liquids move faster than molecules in solids." Ding! Correct! An answer-seeking teacher might be satisfied with the simple contrast regarding the speed of molecules. However, an expert teacher like science teacher Mrs. Amy Miles is interested in how a student processes that information.

Consider what Gabrielle's response reveals when Mrs. Miles poses a follow-up question to Gabrielle's correct answer:

Gabrielle: *Molecules in liquids move faster than molecules in solids.*
Mrs. Miles: *What is an example?*
Gabrielle: *Humans are solids. If I drink a lot of liquid, I will be able to run faster.*

At this point, teachers would notice that the student's response is way off-key. The alarms are screaming in our heads. It's tempting to interject with reteaching the idea of how the distance between molecules determines the state of matter, and how it doesn't have anything to do with the physical movement of the human body. Instead of reteaching, though, ask the student to think about her thinking. Pose a question that uncovers the logic—or illogic, as the case may be. You'll uncover which part of the lesson the student truly understands, and where she's getting confused. Gabrielle revealed where her understanding broke down when attempting to relate physical movement to the state of matter. A masterful educator continues with questions that push Gabrielle's assumptions, and listens for the music of her logic.

> **Once you train yourself to listen for right thinking, you might find yourself saying, "That's music to my ears" in response to student reasoning.**

Gabrielle: *That's because the molecules in the liquid will be moving faster than the rest of my body. Which will make me run faster. That's why my coach tells us to hydrate before track meets. It all makes sense now.*

Mrs. Miles: *You said humans are solid and the water you drink is liquid. Explain your thinking of how running faster connects to the movement of the molecules.*

Gabrielle: *If the molecules in the water mix with the molecules in my body, the slower molecules in my legs will speed up.*

Mrs. Miles: *So they mix together?*

Gabrielle: *Yes.*

Mrs. Miles: *What happens when they're mixed to help your legs speed up?*

Gabrielle: *Hmm, let me think about that. Maybe I'm not right.*

Mrs. Miles: *(pause) What scientific information makes you second-guess your thinking?*

Gabrielle: *If the molecules in my body started moving faster, then my body would turn to liquid, not run faster.*

Mrs. Miles: *What can you conclude from that?*

Gabrielle: *I was thinking that faster molecules would just move faster in every way. But that doesn't really make sense. Now I think that …*

In this exchange, Mrs. Miles heard an alarm. She could see that Gabrielle was over-simplifying the information. She knew yesterday's lesson established a basic knowledge of solids, liquids, and gases, and that Gabrielle was using that knowledge incorrectly. Instead of indicating that Gabrielle's thinking was off, Mrs. Miles used prompts to help the student navigate through the information that was already in her head. The reasoning was in there, but she had not thought it through all the way.

Once you train yourself to listen for right thinking, you might find yourself saying, "That's music to my ears" in response to student reasoning. You will certainly be helping students to refine and utilize their thinking so that it will reach further than giving one right answer.

WHAT YOU CAN DO TOMORROW

It will take rehearsal to retrain the ear to listen for students' thought processes instead of being satisfied with right answers. Before your next lesson, choose one of the following strategies to help you hear the music of students' thinking.

- **Keep an eye on your expert blind spot.** You know what they say happens when you ASS-U-ME? Because many educators have a passion for their content areas, it is easy to forget what it is like not to have so much knowledge. You might see relationships between ideas that freshly exposed learners do not see. What seems obvious to the expert is not always clear to the novice. Look at the content and your lesson through the perspective of a new learner.

Remember, the students do not have the same knowledge that you have, so they don't always see ideas that appear to be in plain view.

Even when you can identify where background knowledge is lacking, it does not work to simply fill in the gaps for students by covering the material. I have had this feeling when the heating and cooling repairman came to my house to fix my air conditioning. About five minutes into his explanation about what was wrong with my unit, I was already lost. His expert blind spot was on high. The evaporator coil is different than the compressor coil and he was checking to see if something froze up. I tried asking clarifying questions, but my gaps were too wide and too plentiful. Then he showed me the lint and debris that had built up inside the unit. I could relate it to how my clothes dryer takes longer to dry clothes when my daughter forgets to clean out the lint trap. The dryer has to work extra hard, just like the A/C unit has to work extra hard. Only my A/C unit had been going at that rate for years. I think he giggled a little when I made my own connection. It wasn't exactly how he was trying to explain it from a technical perspective, but he could see I was "getting it."

Consider the background you have in a content area and try to imagine how you would make sense out of a lesson without all that prior knowledge. What might seem like common sense to you as an expert could be the difference between true understanding and just going through the motions for students. Do not be afraid to state what appears to be obvious. New learners can use the affirmation that they are on the right track and begin to develop their own expertise. Regurgitating information is not music. Students must be able to retrace a cognitive path in a similar but different situation, and that requires thinking, not just answer-getting.

- **Ask the same student two questions in a row.** When a student gives you an answer to a question, follow up with a justification question to prompt the student to articulate his or her thinking. These options for second questions will help reveal the music.

    1. How do you know?
    2. Can you prove it?
    3. What evidence do you have?
    4. What makes you think so?
    5. How can you be sure?

- **Provide think time.** When given the opportunity to extend their thinking, students will often continue to elaborate on their responses without you verbally prompting them. This is an additional benefit to offering think time. Another benefit is that the moments allow you to reflect on what you heard and determine a response. Are you going to affirm a right answer and move on to the next question? Are you going to lower your eyebrows and tilt your head to the side to indicate the student should go back to the drawing board? Keep a poker face and give students and yourself a moment to reflect on what was said. Once you establish the expectation of justifying answers, this moment of silence might be all the students need to play the music for you with their rationales for the answers.

• **Ask metacognitive questions.** We need to listen not only to the music, but also to help students hear the lullaby of their thoughts. Metacognitive questions encourage students to focus on thinking about their own thinking.

Examples:

1. What strategy will you use?
2. What do you already know that will help you?
3. How will you approach the question?
4. What problems might you encounter?
5. What are you trying to achieve?

6. How will you measure success?

7. How will you know if you are wrong?

- **Ask questions about answers.** A sure-fire way to shift students' attention to thinking rather than being limited to just answer-seeking is to give them the answer. Giving correct answers, and answers that are based on misconceptions, allows students to use the answers to explain the thinking behind them. It is powerful to offer both correct and incorrect answers and ask students to justify accurate thinking and assess errors for the purpose of avoiding them in their own work.

A BLUEPRINT FOR FULL IMPLEMENTATION

Step 1: Plan a lesson that has a clear learning purpose.

Whether your district references the purpose of the lesson as learning targets, learning intentions, objectives, or lesson goals doesn't matter. Semantics are less important than having and leveraging them to guide your instructional decisions, including questioning. Maintain a clear focus on what you want students to learn and how you (and they) will know they have learned it. Even in inquiry-based learning, including Next Generation Science Standards (NGSS), the facilitator of the lesson needs to have a purpose in mind. Know what success will look like at the end of a lesson, and you will know what sorts of questions you need to ask students during the journey. You can't hear the music if you don't even know what it's supposed to sound like.

Step 2: Prepare a model with a provided answer.

Select a sample question and provide a correct or incorrect response, depending on what you are trying to reveal. Review the table in Image 8.1 to help you determine which model is best for your lesson.

Provide students with a CORRECT answer if...	So they can...
there are multiple accurate answers	share additional responses identify a criterion to determine the highest quality response
there is primarily one response, but multiple ways to consider it	hear and learn alternate thinking broaden their perspectives
students are learning to justify their reasoning	take the focus off the result and focus on the thinking journey
citing evidence is the focus	prove their answer
emphasis is on a process or procedure	use academic vocabulary to explain how an answer was achieved
Provide students with an INCORRECT answer if...	**So they can...**
a specific mistake is commonly made	recognize incorrect responses identify ways to avoid simple mistakes learn from someone else's mistake
fixed mindsets are prevalent	experience the benefit of learning from errors persevere through challenging ideas or problems
discourse is being taught	practice productive and respectful ways to disagree
analysis is the target	critique the reasoning of others

Image 8.1

Step 3: Identify a few questions that will expose students' logic.

If you don't hear the music, you will have to signal for it. While you're in the planning phase, prepare questions that prompt students to share their thinking process, and keep them in your back pocket. Justification questions such as, "How did you reach that conclusion?" are handy to keep on the tip of your tongue. If students don't routinely offer to show their understanding, use those questions to show them the path.

Step 4: Pose follow-up questions to challenge their thinking.

Use follow-up questions to challenge your students' thought processes. Continuing to pose questions prevents students from halting their thinking once they reach an answer.

1. Are there any exceptions?

2. What problems could occur?

3. Would everyone have the same perspective?

4. Could there be any other solutions?

OVERCOMING PUSHBACK

I know the student gets it. Why should I waste class time making them justify it? You are probably thinking of the student who gives the right answer, and when asked to explain how they reached that conclusion, says, "I just knew." Maybe you had that experience as a learner. In order to be successful in life, though, people need to be able to communicate their thinking to collaborate or persuade others to support them. If they don't learn the speaking skills they need for providing reasoning for their claims, they'll likely be dismissed in future situations. This Hack applies to right answers, wrong answers, and accurate and inaccurate lines of thinking. It's a valuable skill to justify our ideas. Too few students learn how to do it.

If I let students give incorrect reasoning, they will develop misconceptions. If students are articulating their thinking in ways that do not make sense, suppressing their thoughts is not going to prevent misconceptions. The best way to undo a misconception is to address it head-on. Get their logic on the table and dissect it. That path of questioning will often help students realize their own misunderstandings. If they go through their thought process out loud, they are not only more likely to remember it, but also allowed to save face for an incorrect answer. Students who are given the opportunity to rethink for themselves and change their answers build confidence. They are more prone to take cognitive risks in the future. Help students label their misconceptions and figure out what caused the errors in their thinking, so they do not repeat the same wrong thinking.

A sentence stem as simple as: "I used to think _____, because _____. Now I think _____, because _____" provides students with the language to articulate their growth. Routinely prompting students to identify how their understanding of concepts might change after new learning has occurred develops a culture of recognizing mistakes and learning from errors.

The test is not going to look for right thinking, it only cares about right answers. We want to teach to life, not to the test. While there is some truth that the final outcome is what "counts," the idea that we should structure lessons as if they are not a journey goes against the notion of a learning process. If we are only concerned with the right answer from the beginning of the learning experience, we are missing the opportunity for patterns of correct thoughts. We can all remember a time when someone explained their thinking to us, and we had a moment of realization of why they were saying what they were saying. We should be looking for that same clarity when we're listening to student responses. Right thinking leads to right answers, but right answers are not always a result of right thinking.

Other students get bored when one student talks too long. Allow all students to justify their thinking. Teach students to ask for reasoning and justification through the use of accountable talk, such as:

1. How do you know?

2. What is your evidence?

3. Explain your reasoning.

4. Why do you think that?

5. How can you prove it?

A ninety-second Turn and Ask would provide all students the opportunity to share an answer and their justifications. Now you have a classroom of active thinkers rather than passive listeners. In Hack 1: Assume All Hands Are Up, I offered multiple strategies for getting all students to participate in learning. Use them to help students figure out how to think about their thinking during their learning.

THE HACK IN ACTION

Saranac Elementary School is dear to my heart; it has been my professional home for thirteen years, as the principal and now curriculum director. One of the kindergarten teachers there, Mrs. Barbara Cizauskas, is able to get five-year-olds to think hard and communicate clearly about their learning. Sometimes I have to remind myself that it is the first year of formal education for many of these young scholars, because Mrs. Cizauskas makes their learning look so easy. How does she do it? She listens for the music.

A great example of this is how she used questions to listen to correct thinking—not just right answers—during math time. Mrs. Cizauskas was teaching students about the measurable attributes of shapes. This includes length, width, height, weight, and capacity. In a one-on-one exchange with one student, she began exploring ways to measure a tissue box—or as her mathematicians call it, a rectangular prism.

In Images 8.2a–c, the dialogue between Mrs. Cizauskas and Ethan, an at-risk student, is captured in the first column. More important is the description of why she asked each question and what Ethan's reply indicates. You can see how she was able to assist him in thinking without reteaching any of the mathematical concepts they were discussing.

In the question-response process, she heard both music and alarms, but figured out when to question and when to probe.

Moving students from surface understanding to deep understanding is music to our ears. To help us turn that music up, we sometimes have to tune in to thinking and focus less on the answer. Observe how you react to student answers. Remember, the response does not tell you how a student solved a problem or analyzed to reach that solution. Use probing questions to reveal how a student is processing content, and you'll start to hear the music. Stay away from leading questions that allow students to follow your thinking progression instead of developing their own.

The ultimate goal of learning is to maintain knowledge so it can be applied in context and transferred to relevant circumstances. Leading students to the right answer just to celebrate the arrival

	Question/Response	What is the question's purpose?	What is heard in the response?
Q	*What could be measured on this object?*	Assess if he can identify a measurable attribute.	MUSIC: He identified a single attribute.
R	*How wide.*		He didn't use the mathematical term *width*.
Q	*Where would we measure it to show how wide it would be?*	Determine if he can locate the width. Intentionally uses his same words "how wide" and does not replace it with "width"	ALARM: He labeled length and width as the same attribute.
R	*On the sides or in the front. (He points to both)*		
Q	*Is it the same to measure the front and the sides?*	Digging deeper into the misconception that length and width are the same.	MUSIC: He identifies front and back separately from the sides. This exposes a conflict with what he said and how he justified it.
R	*Well the front and the back will get the same. Then this side and this side would be the same.*		
Q	*Hmmm... Are you sure?*	Exposes the level of confidence in his justification.	He is reasonably sure in his thinking. Therefore, clarifying length and width should be relatively easy, but necessary.
R	*Yes. (quickly and without hesitation)*		
Q	*How do you know?*	Reveals the logic behind the claim he made that the front and back are equal.	MUSIC: The connections he is making now are far beyond identifying attributes. This is an opportunity to differentiate beyond the kindergarten level.
R	*Because when you measure it right here (holds the front) it goes the same as right here (turns the box around to the back).*		
Q	*What do we call that measurement? (Pointing to length)*	Returns to the clarification between length and width since initially he said they were "how wide."	ALARM: He labels the length as the width.
R	*How wide it is.*		

Image 8.2a

Question/Response	What is the question's purpose?	What is heard in the response?
Q *So you said the front and the back will have the same measurement and you called it the width. What would you call the sides?* **R** *Ummm...*	Does not give any nonverbal indication that his answer is wrong. Probes to see if he has the terms flip-flopped or doesn't know the difference between length and width.	No response. Maybe he is making meaning.
Q *Pause* **R** *Actually, the front is the length and the sides are how wide.*	Provides time to think	MUSIC: He changes his response and adds the term length to the conversation. He still doesn't say width.
Q *What is the mathematical term we use when we measure how wide something is?* **R** *How wide?*	Checking recall. Does he know "width"?	He is unsure.
Q *If length measures how long something is, what measures how wide something is?* **R** *The width?*	Giving the relationship between two other mathematical terms might cue him to remember "width."	MUSIC: He gives the right answer but doesn't sound confident. Now we want to boost his certainty.
Q *You don't sound sure. Is it the width?* **R** *(Looks at the anchor chart in the classroom) Yes. This is the length (points to front) and this and this (points to sides) is the width.*	Determining if he guessed. Helping him increase his self-confidence.	MUSIC: He used the environment to affirm his thinking. Then clearly articulates length and width using the correct vocabulary.
Q *So let's go back to something you said earlier. You said the length in the front is the same as the length in the back. How can you prove that?* **R** *I can get some tools and show they are the same.*	Now that she has evidence that he met today's target, she returns to the concept of the front and back being equivalent without deviating from the lesson purpose of measurement.	MUSIC: He is eager to prove it. But does not explain what his evidence will be.

Image 8.2b

181

Question/Response	What is the question's purpose?	What is heard in the response?
Q *What tools will help you?*	One of the mathematical practices is to use appropriate tools strategically. This is a chance to exercise that habit.	MUSIC: The tools he chooses are appropriate. "The same" and "equal" are not synonyms in math. Ethan should use accurate vocabulary.
R *Can I go get some unifix cubes? Then I can show it's the same length here and here.*		
Q *What do you mean "the same"?*	Prompting precise language. (Supports math practice: Attend to precision)	ALARM: The term "equal" has been well established in Mrs. Cizauskas's class. He should use it with automaticity.
R *The same length.*		
Q *What is the mathematical term we use when two things have the same value?*	Using a familiar definition helps him to recall the correct term.	MUSIC!
R *Equal.*		
Q *So what are you going to try to prove with your tools? Remember to use math words.*	Clarifying the purpose of his task highlights the learning goal and reduces the chance he will use the tools for play.	He is ready to prove his theory.
R *I am going to prove that the length in the front is the same - I mean equal with the length in the back.*		

Image 8.2c

skips the music altogether. Ask yourself why you are posing a question. Is it simply to find someone who can prove they already knew it? Are you looking for students who might be left behind in the learning? Or is your purpose to analyze what students understand or don't understand yet, and why?

Do you hear music or alarms? Listen closely. Is it coming from right answers … or right thinking?

HACK 9

SCAFFOLD, DON'T SPOON-FEED

TRIGGER STUDENT THINKING WITHOUT DOING IT FOR THEM

It's not what you do for your children, but what you have taught them to do for themselves that will make them successful human beings.

— ANN LANDERS, ADVICE COLUMNIST

THE PROBLEM: TEACHERS SPOON-FEED STUDENTS THE ANSWERS

MOST TEACHERS JOINED the field of education for the students. But the desire to help students become successful is—ironically—what prevents us from doing so. We quickly gain a shortsighted view of learning, and start to think that the measure of success is a single question or completion of a task. Lost is the longer-term and more authentic purpose of instruction: learning.

Many of us are triggered if we see students struggling, and immediately run to support them. Doing so might give them the in-the-moment answer … but it also steals their opportunities to feel a sense of accomplishment.

Instead of providing answers, we need to do something different. Some call it hinting. Others call it providing interventions. It is even labeled in the broad category of questioning. For the purpose of this chapter, we are going to call it scaffolding.

The problem is that most teachers don't use it. They prefer spoon-feeding—to the detriment of student learning. This is perhaps best illustrated with a scene that used to be a daily occurrence in my home. "Mom, where are my shoes?" Here we go again. I would remind myself not to come to the rescue and hunt for the missing shoes. But this single question would set my wheels spinning. I would close my eyes and try to remember if I had seen said sneakers. Coming up blank, I would then consider places I had seen the sneakers in previous instances when they were lost. Back door? Front closet? Under the dinner table? Did you check that messy room of yours?

My daughter would frantically race to search each of the places I suggested until she shouted the glorious cry of "Found them!" Depending on the day, my final comment might be a bit comical, like: "See? Right where you left them." Or it might be a little more direct, like: "If you would just put them away when you take them off, this would not keep happening." This interaction would be closed with the misguided belief that I had held her accountable for finding the sneakers.

Now take a look at the following high school math example: Students are solving the following inequality: $8n - 2 > 17n + 16$. One student is stuck, so he raises his hand for the teacher to come over. When she does, the following dialogue occurs:

Teacher: *What seems to be the problem?*
Student: *I don't get it.*
Teacher: *What have you tried so far?*
Student: *Nothing. I am not sure where to start.*
Teacher: *Okay, the first step is to combine like terms.*
Student: *...*
Teacher: *So we have to get the Ns on one side.*
Student: *<grabs a pencil>*
Teacher: *If there is 8n on this side and 17n on the other side, how do we get them both on the same side?*
Student: *We move one of them.*
Teacher: *Right. So if we subtract 8n from the left, what do we have to do to the right?*
Student: *The same thing.*
Teacher: *Yes! You're getting it. So what's 17n minus 8n?*
Student: *9?*
Teacher: *Nine what?*
Student *9n.*
Teacher: *<high fives student> I think you are set. Keep going and I'll come back and check on you.*

Clue number one that you're spoon-feeding more than properly scaffolding: Who's doing most of the talking?

Clue number one that you're spoon-feeding more than properly scaffolding: Who's doing most of the talking?

The purpose of this lesson was to solve inequalities. The line of questioning the teacher offered provoked mathematical thinking around simple subtraction of like terms. It was actually the teacher who paved the path for the student to solve the problem. The likelihood that this student will be able to independently solve the next problem is not increased by much as a result of this exchange.

We all want to experience that moment when we've created an *aha* moment for a student. In an effort to do so, we interact to try to trigger thinking. Sometimes too soon, and sometimes way too much. The problem with spoon-feeding in this way is that it gives everyone a false sense of learning. You might have led students to water so they could drink, but that does not mean they can return to the water source and drink again another day without you.

You need to change your method of scaffolding and teach them how to build the map they need to use to get to that water again. Teach them how to do it for themselves instead of doing it for them.

THE HACK: SCAFFOLD, DON'T SPOON-FEED

When I discovered the power of using a sequence of prompts instead of cues, it was life-changing. I am no longer asked several times a week where to find *anything*. I used what I know about scaffolding to trigger self-questioning in my forgetful teen.

What does this mean? Scaffolding is a chronological sequence of questions that supports students when they need it—and shows them how to do it again. See Image 9.1 for the sequence for scaffolding.

Question: This might be one of your Broken Record questions (see Hack 5). No matter what the question, it should reveal what the student does or does not yet know in relation to the learning target.

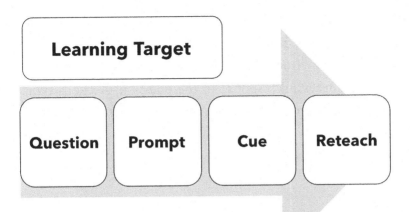

Image 9.1

Prompt: This should send the learner back into their own head to search for information they can use to respond to the question. A prompt triggers cognitive or metacognitive thinking for the learner. Metaphorically, you're turning a light on in a dark room to allow the students an opportunity to "see" for themselves. If you

CAUTION: IT'S A COMMON ERROR FOR EDUCATORS TO DRAW CONCLUSIONS WHEN A STUDENT RESPONDS ACCURATELY TO A PROMPT OR CUE. ONLY USE A PROMPT OR CUE WHEN A STUDENT IS UNABLE TO THINK THROUGH IT INDEPENDENTLY. AVOID THE INTERPRETATION THAT A SUCCESSFUL RESPONSE MEANS LEARNING WILL TRANSFER TO SIMILAR SITUATIONS.

filled your back pocket with questions (see Hack 6), you should have a few of these ready.

Cue: This is a visual, verbal, or kinesthetic signal that leads students to a successful response to the question. A cue is typically external and narrows the resources for students. Cues shine a flashlight on where students should look when simply turning the light on is not enough.

Question	Reteach
Mom, where are my shoes?	You left them on the stairs. That's not where they belong. Next time put them in the closet.

Image 9.2

Reteach: This means repetition or modeling of the initial learning. You can repeat it the way you originally shared it, or use an alternate presentation of the information. Reteaching alone has a very low level of cognitive accountability for the student.

Image 9.2 reflects the scenario described in the problem section of this Hack. The end result is that she found the shoes. But if I continue to use this same sequence to provide an answer, along with a reminder of a preventive solution, the cycle will repeat itself any time something is missing. Sure, if she had just put the item where it belonged, this wouldn't be a problem. Focusing on how to prevent it, though, does nothing to assist my daughter when something is lost. When a book turns up missing, you can bet I'm going to hear, "Mom, where is my book?"

Inserting cues in place of a direct explanation ensures that my daughter makes *some* effort to find her shoes. However, her mental process is still:

1. Ask Mom.

2. Look where Mom suggests.

3. If the shoes are not there, return to step one.

Question	**Cues**
Mom, where are my shoes?	Have you checked all the doors? Did you leave them at school again? Are they somewhere in your room?

Image 9.3

Transferring the exact cues in Image 9.3 will send my daughter to look for her shoes by the front and back door, at school, and in her room. If she left the shoes in the car, these cues offer no help. Coming up empty-handed will just encourage her to return to me for more cues.

In the following example, though, where a student might be learning to understand why authors write a text, we see a different scaffolding. In the example, the student has completed a formative assessment that indicated that he clearly understood that authors write to inform, persuade, or entertain. He was also able to independently give a definition or example of each in his own words. Today, his teacher is having him apply his knowledge to a text. He was tasked with reading a text and then determining why the author wrote it. This is a scaffolding sequence with only one example for each step. Image 9.4 is an example of a scaffolded learning target.

Learning Target
Determine author's purpose of a nonfiction article.

Question
What is the author's purpose of this text?

Prompt
What are some reasons authors write?

Cue
What does the first line of the second paragraph tell you about why the author wrote this article?

Reteach
When you see "everyone should..." that doesn't inform or entertain. So what is the author's purpose?

Image 9.4

This is one sequence of scaffolding, and you can add to it. Don't miss the opportunity to keep the cognitive demand high by using multiple prompts before moving to cues. One of the biggest causes of spoon-feeding is moving on with additional support too soon. In a perfect world, we wouldn't need prompts or cues because students would independently scaffold themselves. Until they are capable of applying their own prompts and cues, though, the teacher temporarily steps into that role.

Here is an example of how Lawrence's teacher uses only prompts, then returns to the question repeatedly to determine if each prompt was successful:

Question: *What is the author's purpose for writing this article?*

Lawrence: *Video games and reading.*

Question: *<reworded and including his previous response> Why did the author write this article about video games and reading?*

Lawrence: *The author is probably a teacher.*

Prompt: *If the author were a teacher, what do you think his purpose was for writing this article?*

Lawrence: *Huh?*

Prompt: *What are the reasons authors write?*

Lawrence: *To inform, persuade, or entertain.*

Question: *<reworded to include his words> So is this author's purpose for writing this article to inform, persuade, or entertain?*

Lawrence: *To tell kids they should read as much as they play video games.*

Prompt: *Of the three purposes you just told me, which one does that message suggest?*

Lawrence: *Persuade.*

Question: *So what is the author's purpose for writing this article?*

Lawrence: *The author wrote this article to persuade kids to read more. Persuade.*

In the case of the lost shoes, when I began to provide prompts, it was my daughter who mentally searched for possible solutions. I just gave her a little guidance about how to problem-solve without doing it for her.

Question	Prompts
Mom, where are my shoes?	Retrace your steps. Where have you looked? How did you find them last time?

Image 9.5

You can transfer the cognitive prompts offered in Image 9.5 to a lost book or glasses. For younger children, this mental reflection can help them find a favorite toy, too. Granted, it would be better if they stopped losing items in the first place. But just in case an absentminded son or daughter, or student, neglects to put everything in its proper place, use prompts to allow them to trigger their own thinking and move toward being more independent.

Let's revisit the math exchange from the beginning of the chapter. This time, the teacher uses questioning that triggers thinking for the student and maintains an appropriate level of rigor for this lesson:

Prompt: *What seems to be the problem?*
Student: *I don't get it.*
Prompt: *What have you tried so far?*
Student: *Nothing. I am not sure where to start.*
Prompt: *Okay. Think back to the example we did together.*
Student: *I don't remember.*
Prompt: *What was the first thing we did? I think it was Justin who started us off.*
Student: *He got the Ws on the same side.*
Prompt: *Why would that help?*

Student: *To make it easier to graph. Like n < 5 is easier than this one.*

Prompt: *So what are you going to do first in this problem?*

Student: *Move the Ns to the same side.*

Prompt: *How are you going to decide which side?*

Student: *I'm going to move the 8n to the right so I don't have to deal with negative numbers.*

Prompt: *I can see why you might want to make that choice. Now what?*

Student: *I'm not sure. I'm stuck again.*

Prompt: *What resources do you have to help you when you're stuck?*

Student: *Only my calculator, but that's not going to help.*

Cue: *What about your notes?*

Student: *Oh yeah. I see what Justin did because I wrote it down right here. I've got it from here.*

Reflection Question: *Looking back to when you were stuck, what seemed to help you get through it?*

Student: *When I started thinking about how to make the problem easier to graph, then I knew what to do. I'm also glad I took good notes because that helped me too.*

Reflection Question: *So how can you use that reflection to help you in the future?*

Student: *I just need to ask myself, "Is there a way I can make this easier?" If that doesn't work, then I can look at my notes to remind me.*

This line of questioning focuses on the process of solving an inequality and the reason for the step, not the arithmetic of subtracting terms. The teacher even saw an opportunity for the student to reflect on what triggered the *aha* moment to capture that awareness and tuck it away for future use.

WHAT YOU CAN DO TOMORROW

Getting out of the habit of using questions to spoon-feed takes quite a bit of practice. Here are ways to help you recognize where you might help too much, and suggestions for building a routine of sequential scaffolding.

- **Record yourself asking questions.** Capture a five-minute video of a portion of a lesson, small-group instruction, or individual coaching time with a student. Choose a time when scaffolding is involved. Watch the video and identify your questions, prompts, cues, or reteaching. Pay special attention to any times you might even answer your own question.

- **Sequence your Broken Record questions.** As you get more accustomed to identifying Broken Record questions, tie them to scaffolding. Label them as questions, prompts, or cues. Then keep them in order. Resist using cues unless you have evidence that the prompts are not offering enough support.

- **Make a list of prompts you are already using.** Most of us have questions we keep in our back pockets. If you make a conscious effort to increase how often you're using prompts, you'll align your scaffolding more accurately with the appropriate support. Never give more than necessary. Image 9.6 offers a list of the prompts most frequently heard in classrooms.

PROMPTS

- What do you already know?
- What strategy can you use?
- What is the question asking you?
- What information have you learned?
- How are you going to approach this?
- What are you thinking or considering?
- Is that logical?
- Does it make sense?
- What do you need to figure out?
- Where can you begin your thinking?
- What does this remind you of?
- How can you help yourself get unstuck?
- What did you learn from your group?
- How can you remember?
- Where can you get more information?
- What information do you need?

Image 9.6

Delineate between prompts and cues. Listen to how you scaffold. Be sure you are not using prompts and cues as if they are the same. There is a subtle difference in the following questions, and no difference in the actual student behavior.

- **What resources might help you?**
  This question prompts the student to engage in metacognition. The student has to think about the problem and possible resources, then identify whether those resources are available. Use this prompt and you will be close to the student not needing any scaffolding. This is only one step away from self-prompting instead of depending on the teacher to initiate the process.

- **What does the example on the board tell you?**
  This cue triggers compliance. The teacher knows that the example on the board is similar to the example the student is facing, and will likely assist the student with where to go next. Granted, the student still has to interpret the example on the board, so it is not completely spoon-feeding. The problem with skipping the prompt and landing on the cue is that it removes any independence. The student was not prompted to consider how to help herself.

A BLUEPRINT FOR FULL IMPLEMENTATION

Step 1: Develop a learning resource collectively with students.

When you are planning a unit, make a note of components that are likely to be a struggle for students or that require more than the average amount of support as students are mastering it. Design resources to help students around those issues. The list in Image 9.7 offers examples of common resources. These will help students until they have built a sound understanding and are ready to become independent. Use these resources as cues when and if you need them.

Anchor charts	Graphic organizers	Mentor texts
Annotations	Highlighted text	Mnemonics
Body movement	Jingles	Notes
Environmental print	Manipulatives	Visual aids
Gestures	Maps	Worked examples

Image 9.7

Step 2: During active learning, use your Broken Record to assess progress.

Here's where the Hacks are coming together and supporting your ability to implement your process. Hack 8 highlighted how to listen to the music. In your lessons, you will be listening for right thinking, evidence of student misconceptions, or gaps in understanding. In order to solicit this evidence, begin with the Broken Record as your question. If students are able to give a response that illustrates that they have grasped a skill, concept, or idea beyond just the right answer, celebrate. If not, move to step three.

Step 3: If students need support, use prompts.

Many teachers have a handful of prompts they leave in their sight so they can have them handy when it is time to initiate a scaffold to reinforce previous learning. This is a realistic option since many prompts are not content- or lesson-specific. Asking students how they are going to organize their thought process is applicable to any content area—and will help students in their learning journeys.

Step 4: If prompts are not working, use a cue.

Since you have prepared resources to serve as cues, you will not be limited if you exhaust your prompts. A natural lead before giving a cue is to offer one last prompt, such as:

- What resources might help you?
- What tools are available to you that might be useful?
- Where could you go to get more information or support?
- What aids did you use when you were initially learning about this?

All of these prompts have the potential to eliminate the need for a cue. If they do not trigger the student to identify a resource, then move on to offering a cue. You can signal a cue in a few different ways, as outlined in Image 9.8.

Step 5: If you have to reteach, give the baton to the student.

From time to time, for various reasons, learning might not stick. All the prompting and cueing in the world sends the teacher and student round and round, but they still get nowhere. Reteaching or providing background knowledge to fill the gaps seems like a daily occurrence. But it's often a needed one. It is important to note that if students didn't catch on the first time, simply telling them will lead to one probable result: They won't catch on the second time, either. In the future, use a scaffold to increase the likelihood that students will retain the information. Do this by choosing an action that hands over the baton to them.

Verbal Cues

- Repeat student's response with a question tone
- Restate only the point to be made
- Slow down or put inflection on words/phrases to draw attention to them
- Stop a sentence before a key word to cue students to the word

Visual Cues

- Anchor chart
- Graphic organizer
- Images
- Various text features
- Environmental resources like word bank or procedure
- Manipulatives

Kinesthetic Cues

- Gestures that convey meaning
- isolating a specific portion of a text or resource by covering other parts
- Pointing to where students should look or go without saying it
- Using body motions that were modeled in a lesson

Image 9.8

Admittedly, these are somewhat low-level strategies of accountability, but they improve upon what rushed and exhausted teachers resort to—which is no accountability at all. Image 9.9 illustrates that some accountability is better than none.

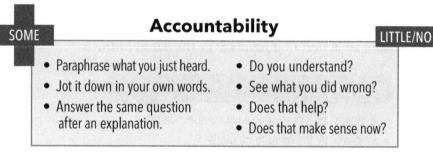

Image 9.9

OVERCOMING PUSHBACK

Lightening the amount of scaffolding you are providing for students might be the most difficult Hack to master. It can be difficult to harmonize students' confidence and feelings of safety with an appropriate level of challenge. You'll receive pushback from educators who don't see the value in it.

If I give that many prompts and cues, I will lose the rest of the class's attention. Scaffolding doesn't have to happen immediately. If you are having a class discussion and you notice that a student requires scaffolding, delay it until you can work with that student one-on-one or in a smaller group. The use of prompts and cues is very individual, so unless you are reinforcing a questioning sequence or modeling the use of a tool for many students, it might be better to hold off rather than using the general learning time to individualize for one.

If they don't know, they don't know. Prompts and cues won't help. In the end, this might be true for a specific circumstance.

Prompting offers more than the single outcome of getting to a right answer today, though. Model perseverance and a growth mindset when faced with a struggle to establish it as the norm, not the convenient exception. Besides, you will never know if a prompt could have provoked connections unless you try. Remember to let the evidence (and the students) speak for itself to avoid making assumptions.

Sometimes I can tell they don't know and I feel like I should reteach. In these moments when you are focused so intently on content, pause. Shift your wondering away from the learning target for a moment and search for the bigger picture. It is impossible to teach students everything they need to know. The empowered student knows how to learn. The more you expose them to successful prompting, the more routine it becomes. Then your learners will prompt themselves and exemplify the lifelong skills to own their learning.

THE HACK IN ACTION

The best fifty-eight minutes I ever spent watching a teacher not teach was in Ms. Laura Sloma's high school physics class. She pridefully monitored students as they mirrored her talent for prompting. Prior to the lesson, Ms. Sloma told us her goal was to summarize what the students had learned about constant velocity motion. One agreement her class developed was that students would share information with each other. They also requested a review or study sheet before tests.

When we visited her classroom on October 2, only about one month into the school year, she was initiating a gradual process of turning the task of creating a study guide over to the students. She wanted to teach them how to identify the key points and document them in a way that would be a helpful resource. Ms. Sloma knew that the actual development of the study guide would probably be more beneficial than possessing the completed sheet. She kept that thought to herself.

She explained that she was going to begin by providing them with a template. As the year moved on, her goal was to transition the template over to a completely blank sheet of paper. The day her peers and I observed her classroom, she was introducing this idea to her students. She began the lesson by greeting students and inquiring briefly about their weekend. When she moved into assigning the challenge of using a template to create their own study guide, she was only six minutes into the class period.

Normally when I observe in a classroom, I try to equalize my attention between what the teacher is doing and what students are doing. In Ms. Sloma's class, I was seated close to two different groups of young scientists. For the rest of the class period, I listened to their conversations. There was no need to listen to her because she was invisible. I scripted much of their discussion for the purpose of sharing it with Ms. Sloma when we debriefed her lesson. I wrote down a number of quotes from the teens that would have doubled as prompts. It was the best music.

In the handful of weeks they had been attending her class, they picked up on the techniques she used to scaffold. At one point during class, one of the groups began to question themselves. They struggled with one of the concepts around velocity and could not agree. A group member raised her hand. I could see that Ms. Sloma saw the hand go up. I also noticed that she took her sweet time finding her way to their table. Something I watch for in observations is what students do during the time between when they begin to seek help from the teacher and when that help arrives. I watched that precise process unfold.

The students in this group continued to talk and get clarity about their question. Even the student with her hand up actively participated in the group discussion. At one point, her arm got tired from holding it up and she heavily sighed and switched arms. Her friend in the group said, "I don't even know why you have your hand up. You know she's not going to tell us. She's just gonna come over here and give you another question to your question. We can do that without her." Another student commented on how she was tired of waiting and they should just ask questions like Ms. Sloma does until they could figure it out.

While all this talk was happening, I caught Ms. Sloma's eyes glancing over at this table long enough for me to suspect she was listening to them. Still, she made no effort to hustle over to them. Then the magic happened. These high school students began to repeatedly prompt themselves, and it worked! They were able to talk themselves right into understanding the learning target: *I can analyze constant velocity motion using position vs. time graphs, velocity vs. time graphs, motion maps, and written descriptions.*

At the end of class, I took a moment to speak to the student who raised her hand.

Student: *She will never just give us an answer.*
Me: *How do you feel about that?*
Student: *Personally, I'm frustrated at first, but I know what's she's doing.*
Me: *Does it work?*
Student: *Well, yeah. I like working in a group.*
Me: *What if she had given you the study guide and said, "Here, study this on your own."*
Student: *Oh, that wouldn't work because I wouldn't do it. This is way better.*

Me: *So, did you need her help?*
Student: *Actually no. We're a pretty good group. We like to learn from each other. Ms. Sloma would be proud. We kinda go into teacher mode with each other, ya know?*

And … drop mic!

The paramount difference between a prompt and a cue is the step of sending the student back inside their own head before offering a specific direction to look or think. As the Hack in Action illustrates, moving from teacher-provided prompts to students prompting themselves means a smoother transition. The ability to cue oneself requires an individual to be aware of what learning is missing and how to fill that gap. The reflections of "What am I missing?" and "How might I fill my gaps?" are metacognitive prompts in themselves. Students who are able to ask themselves these questions in challenging moments are more likely to overcome their challenges without needing additional outside support.

Spoon-feeding is almost always a sign of answer-seeking. Remember that scaffolding, both literally and figuratively, is temporary. If students are only able to achieve success with excessive support from you, and are then unable to be independently successful, the scaffold becomes a permanent crutch.

HACK 10

SPIN THE THROTTLE
FUEL STUDENTS TO ASK THE QUESTIONS

*My mother made me a scientist without ever intending
to. Every other Jewish mother in Brooklyn would ask
her child after school, "So? Did you learn anything
today?" But not my mother. "Izzy," she would say, "did
you ask a good question today?" That difference—
asking good questions—made me become a scientist.*

— ISIDOR ISAAC RABI, PHYSICIST, NOBEL PEACE PRIZE WINNER

THE PROBLEM: TEACHERS ASK ALL THE QUESTIONS

WE SEEM TO place a heavy emphasis on teachers crafting and delivering high-quality questions. Until now, even this book has been focused on what questions to ask and when—and mainly teacher to student. When the teacher is the source of the questioning, it means we're still withholding ownership of the learning from the student. We cannot fully transfer the drive for learning to students if we maintain control of all the questions.

Businesses value employees who can ask questions to push their establishments to continuously improve. Memes and tweets galore exist that communicate the value of one's ability to ask the right question over the ability to regurgitate an answer. States require districts to teach speaking and listening skills that include the ability to ask and answer questions with complexity, purpose, and depth. Yet the number of academic questions students are generating is a fraction of those asked by teachers. Even those inquiries typically fall into the clarifying category rather than interpretive or cognitive.

If we expect students to become seasoned in the art of questioning, we have to hand over the cognitive baton and let them run with it.

When we create opportunities for students to craft questions, we often hear questions that are absurdly broad or ridiculously narrow. The most common student questions are those they pose to their peers, like, "What do you think?" This vague question suggests little intentionality from the asker and invites an unspecific response like, "It's good." Alternately, the microscopic view shows us questions that are often closed, such as, "Is this one right?" or "How do you spell ____?" These very specific questions trigger responses that expire. The answer given by the peer is only useful for this exact activity, assignment, or problem. The potential to spark a lightbulb in the future, even in a similar scenario, is miniscule.

Some teachers are able to teach students to pose questions in the sweet spot on the specificity continuum. The next barrier is encouraging students to think of multiple questions to critique their own brainstorms and determine which questions are best and why, before settling on one.

THE HACK: SPIN THE THROTTLE

There is a time for the teacher to activate learning, and there is a time to fuel students to activate their own learning. Questions are an effective way to bring about that learning. Spinning the throttle puts students in the driver's seat when it comes to asking questions. But it is not as simple as just tasking students to generate great questions. Without intentional and specific learning about questions, they will produce low-quality questions. Students will not learn to inquire like Socrates merely through exposure to teachers and parents presenting hundreds of questions every day.

If we expect students to become seasoned in the art of questioning, we have to hand over the cognitive baton and let them run with it.

If you want your students to become good questioners, you need to teach them about questions. As you implement the Hacks, you will undoubtedly improve your own inquiry. Eventually, students will begin to emulate your questions in their own circles. You'll be excited when they start building their own asking skills, and you can actually rev that throttle by explicitly addressing how to write, critique, and pose questions.

I have found two powerful methods to be most effective in energizing those abilities. The first is Right Question Institute's (rightquestion.org) systematic process called the Question Formulation Technique (QFT). They developed this to teach students to produce quality questions. The second is a tight protocol called reciprocal teaching, which offers the structure for students to ask questions with ample opportunity for differentiation. Trust these approaches to help you spin the throttle.

QFT highlights the value of quality questions. It intentionally teaches students how to improve their inquiries. The process invites students to critique and analyze questions before using them to drive their investigations. Students are deeply committed to these driving questions because they have developed them by building on other questions they've derived, then selected them as the best questions to guide their learning endeavor.

Reciprocal teaching is a collaborative learning structure that assigns a role to each student to aid in the comprehension of a text. These roles include:

Summarizer: Periodically pauses the reading to check for understanding and recap what was read.

Questioner: Brings details and wonderings about the text to the surface.

Clarifier: Notes portions of the text that might be confusing or unknown to the readers and helps make sense of them.

Predictor: Uses background knowledge of content and text structure to forecast what the author will share next.

See Image 10.1 for examples of questions under each role in a reciprocal teaching framework.

Beginning in the third grade, most states have a speaking and listening standard that requires students to come to conversations prepared. Being ready to engage in collaborative conversations includes considering the individual group member's questions about the learning. Each student can also prepare for discourse by planning questions that push the group's thinking. Arm students with the skills to design thoughts and questions. Use the lens of

Summarizer	• How could we recap this part? • What are the key points so far? • What is the big idea in this section? • What word best describes what we know at this point?
Questioner	• What information do we have? • What connections can we make? • What details are important to note? • What theme or pattern is emerging?
Clarifier	• What is confusing or unclear? • What wonderings do we have? • How is new vocabulary used? • How does this compare to predictions we made?
Predictor	• How can we determine what might come next? • What predictions do we have? • What clues do we have to help us think ahead? • How will we check our predictions?

Image 10.1

the comprehension roles from reciprocal teaching to fuel their dialogue rather than showing and telling the answers to the group.

With the four reciprocal teaching roles in mind, start off by offering sample questions that align with each role. Then, as students get cruising with the Question Formulation Technique, ask them to replace the summarizer, clarifier, questioner, and predictor questions with ones they write themselves. This combination is sure to get their conversations moving.

WHAT YOU CAN DO TOMORROW

Toddlers naturally ask questions, and a lot of them. But school can turn questions into less interesting discussions. Tap into the toddler in your students by trying these approaches, and see whether you can bring back their inquisitive sides.

- **Let wonderings marinate.** Don't feel like every question has to be addressed the moment a student asks it. When students ask you a question, unless it's needed for immediate clarification, give it status by allowing it to linger for a while. Maybe even days. Extending the length of a wondering can help build stamina—or start independent questioning. Too often, students (and adults, for that matter) are quick to give up on a question if they don't get an immediate answer. How long do you wrestle with a question before pulling out your phone and doing a web search to curb your curiosity? I bet it's well under a minute. Instead of bringing closure to a natural interest, circle back to it. Reject any encouragement to look it up. More satisfaction exists in figuring something out on your own than consulting the internet, and the same is true for your students. Give them a chance to wonder about it for a while, and see whether they come up with answers on their own.

- **Launch a lesson by brainstorming questions.** Establishing a mindset for learning is a useful way to prime students for a new lesson. Instead of activating prior knowledge about an idea or topic, change it up by inviting students to generate questions about it. Take the traditional KWL chart (knows, wants to know, has learned) and hack it. QKAN (questions, knowledge, answers, next steps) now guides your unit.

  > What QUESTIONS do you have?
  > What KNOWLEDGE or strategies do you have to answer the questions?
  > What ANSWERS do you already have?
  > What are your NEXT steps to fill in gaps, confirm your thinking, or go deeper?

- **Show your own curiosity.** When a wondering pops into your head, share it. Illustrate how your mind is naturally curious, and how inquiry is a way of daily life.

- **Let some inquiries go unanswered.** There are two reasons to leave things hanging. One, if out-of-sequence learning progressions will cause misconceptions, do not address them (yet). Two, if a teachable moment will jeopardize today's learning and you determine it is not worth the sacrifice, put an inquiry in a parking lot and return to it another day.

- **Compare questions.** Talk about the semantics, clarity, and purpose of questions. When you ask a question that needs revision, take the opportunity now and again to articulate why one question was not effective and why the rephrased question is better. As students pose what might be labeled as a "good question," give feedback as to why the question is labeled as such.

A BLUEPRINT FOR FULL IMPLEMENTATION

The following steps align with the Question Formulation Technique (QFT), developed by Dan Rothstein and Luz Santana of the Right Question Institute.

Step 1: Design a Question Focus (QFocus).

The first step of QFT requires the most effort. The QFocus is the item that will spark student questioning. Choose a quote, statement, image, math problem, book cover, or anything else, but never make your QFocus a question. The best QFocus is simple enough to be clear, yet complex enough to trigger natural wonderings. Image 10.2 illustrates how a quote could serve as a QFocus, like this one from Malcolm X. Image 10.3 shows how a piece of art might be used to spark inquiry in students. (The drawing is a public domain image that shows the burying of Union dead on the Antietam battlefield in 1862.) Image 10.4 illustrates a math QFocus and the questions young children might ask about this image.

Image 10.2

Image 10.3

Image 10.4

Step 2: Introduce the rules of QFT.

The QFT process includes only four rules. They seem simple enough, but students will probably need help sticking to them, and will be tempted to break them. Not because the students are being defiant, but because it is natural to reflect on questions when interacting with them. Answering questions during the QFT is a violation of one of the rules.

> Rule 1: Ask as many questions as you can.
> Rule 2: Do not stop to discuss, judge, or answer the questions.
> Rule 3: Write down every question exactly as it is stated.
> Rule 4: Change any statement into a question.

Follow this step every time the QFT process is used. Do not assume that students know the rules because they had to follow them the last time a QFT was led. This is an important part of the entire sequence. Allow students to reflect on the following questions.

- What might be difficult about following the rules for producing questions?

- Which rule might be most difficult to follow?

Step 3: Introduce the Question Focus and produce questions.

Designate a recorder and give students chart paper and markers. As the group starts to rattle off questions related to the QFocus, have the recorder record and number the questions. Give students a time limit. Five minutes is a good starting point. Adjust the allotted time as needed to enable students to produce fifteen to thirty-five questions. Remind them to follow the rules. This is the step that makes spinning the throttle visible. You will be able to watch and listen to the questions they brainstorm. The chart paper filled with questions makes it possible for students to see their thoughts.

Step 4: Improve questions.

After time is up, task students with categorizing questions as open or closed. If they are unfamiliar with these types of questions, do a mini lesson on open/closed questions before starting a QFT. In their groups, have students write a C after a question if it can be answered with yes/no or a one-word/short phrase answer. Closed questions usually have a single right answer. Open questions, on the other hand, produce more detailed explanations and often have more than one perspective.

Once each question is labeled as open or closed, ask students to discuss the value of open- and closed-ended questions. An inaccurate assumption is that open-ended questions are unilaterally better than closed. This is not true. At times, you need a concise and specific answer to provide definitive clarity to your inquiry. For example, asking my grandma, "Why don't my cookies taste as good as yours?" is less effective than a closed-ended question: "What's the secret ingredient in your cookies?"

Next, students can select one closed-ended question and improve upon it by making it open. Then find one open-ended question and improve on it by spinning it to closed.

Step 5: Prioritize questions.

Be sure students are clear about how they will use their questions. Certain questions are better for discussion than for conducting research, or preparing an informational presentation. This next step guides students to choose the top three questions that will be most helpful for the project or activity. Start with three, but use your judgment. If five questions will give students more direction in their project-based learning (PBL), then go with five. The number of prioritized questions is less important than the process of prioritizing.

Verbalizing the criteria students used to complete this step is essential to the learning of developing quality questions. All students within the group should be able to explain the reasoning for why the prioritized questions rose to the top as the best.

Step 6: Discuss the next steps.

Now that students have identified their best questions, they can develop a plan of action. Prompt them to discuss how they will use these questions. When students are fueled to ask their own questions, they improve the following activities:

- Conduct an experiment.

- Provide guidance for research.

- Introduce a topic.

- Generate interest in a unit of study.

- Identify driving questions for a project.

- Prepare for a class visitor or meeting.

- Plan for a debate or discussion.

- Make predictions.

- Closely observe a complex visual.

Keep adding to the list as you and your students find more ways to put their questions to good use.

Step 7: Reflect.

Direct students to consider what they learned and how they can use it. This brings their attention to the process of formulating questions. Reflection questions might include:

1. What do you notice about where your top three questions were generated in your brainstorming sequence?

2. How did asking questions help you learn?

3. What did you discover by using the QFT?

4. What surprised you about this process?

5. What might you do differently in your future learning now that you have experienced QFT?

OVERCOMING PUSHBACK

Questioning is often perceived as a teacher's role. Turning students into effective questioners means changing the role inquiry plays in the learning process. Instead of questions feeling like a gotcha, spinning the throttle invites students to appreciate the usefulness of questions. But you will get pushback on this idea.

Speaking and listening skills are ELA standards and I teach a different subject. Speaking and listening are life skills necessary for success in all areas. The more intentional we are with giving students opportunities to grow in these areas, the better communicators they will become. QFT, inquiry, and conversational exchanges of Q&A are beneficial in any class.

Asking questions does not help students get answers. Without questions, there would be no answers. They are directly related.

Posing questions generates the inspiration to seek solutions. Encouraging curiosity and wonder is a way to motivate and inspire.

A QFT lesson takes a long time. The QFT is not executed in isolation. In step six, I go over the purpose of using the QFT process, which is to bring relevance to the task. As with anything new, it might take longer the first couple of times. Activate students to consider the quality of a question, then critique its value. They will connect to the question and develop a determination to follow up and resolve it.

It's like pulling teeth to get students to answer. How am I ever going to get them to ask questions? When Q&A is separated to look solely at questions first, there is something freeing about not having to answer them. Some students get tense with the idea that someone might ask them a question. A way to ease the pressure of Q&A is to recognize and celebrate quality questions. When inquiry is viewed as a genuine desire to learn, questions become appreciated rather than feared.

If I allow students to generate questions, they won't be deep enough. That's exactly the inspiration for this Hack. Initially, you will have to struggle with simple questions. The purpose of spinning the throttle is to put students in the position of taking the next step. Analyze the quality of the questions, and help students build on that quality.

THE HACK IN ACTION

In a meeting before Mrs. Paula Warren was scheduled to be observed, she asked the CIFT members if there were any strategies we desired to see in action or wanted her to try. Among the requests was to see an introduction of reciprocal teaching in action. Mrs. Warren viewed it as a way to improve her already solid pedagogy. This willingness to attempt something she had never tried before, while five other educators watched, was an indication of how committed she was to her professional growth. We embraced the opportunity for feedback. She accepted the challenge to implement reciprocal teaching.

The first time the CIFT visited Mrs. Warren's class, her high schoolers were reading *Macbeth*, a Shakespearean tragedy. William Shakespeare is a challenging read for many students, and because of the text's complexity, it was a perfect fit for the reciprocal teaching protocol. First, she introduced students to the protocol itself. She showed a brief video that introduced the steps and, more important, the roles. In this lesson, she assigned the roles with color-coded sheets of paper. Since the protocol was new to students, Mrs. Warren printed out springboard questions for each role. She made these copies on four different-colored sheets of paper, each representing summarizer, clarifier, questioner, or predictor.

Before launching students into the text, she notified them that she was going to carry a clipboard. On the clipboard, she was going to take notes about how the protocol was working. After the lesson, she would invite them to share their thoughts about reciprocal teaching and she would share her observations from their first attempt with it. Mrs. Warren had never tried this process and was unsure about how it would go. Her decision to communicate that in advance hinted that there was an expectation that they'd need to tweak things after the first time through.

Immediately, it was evident that students were excited to read in groups. As they gathered their materials in preparation to read scene four, Mrs. Warren handed out their assigned roles. We heard one student share with a peer, "I definitely want the questioner." All students read the first section independently, through the lens of their assigned task. Each student annotated the text, and some referred back to the sample questions their teacher had provided.

The structure of the roles, along with the provided resource, supported students as they aided one another in comprehending the text. Since this was their first time following a reciprocal teaching protocol, students would sometimes slip into a free-flowing conversation. Usually without a reminder from Mrs. Warren, someone in the group would advise them to stay true to their roles. An unanticipated action that occurred in more than one group happened when a student had trouble executing an assigned role. For example, in one group, the summarizer was having a hard time comprehending the main points. A peer sat straight in his seat and announced, "I'm the clarifier, so it would go to me to clarify that. Basically, the main point is ... "

Questions and ideas swirled in every group. If a lull occurred in the dialogue, someone would reference the sample questions and get the conversation rolling again. The lesson unfolded even better than anticipated. When it came time to debrief, one person suggested to include a time manager role. Someone needed to watch the clock, but it was not a reading role. The priority of the protocol was for each student to be engaged in reading and bring interactions to the table. In most of the groups, the summarizer was the one who could take on the added task of keeping track of monitoring time.

About ten months later, it was Mrs. Warren's turn to host another lesson. She was getting crazy with the use of protocols. This time, she distributed neon sunglasses of various colors. When students led a group discussion, they had to do it through a predetermined "lens." Great pun, Paula. Your students loved it!

I recently shared the Question Formulation Technique with a group of high school teachers, and their observation about the process was enlightening. Four groups of teachers each had a different QFocus to generate their questions. One of the images was an intricate piece of art with excessive detail in both the focal point and the background. The painting was open for interpretation. Another one was a simple photograph of a sloth climbing a tree.

When given the option for which QFocus they wanted, the first group chose the simple picture, leaving the more complex visuals for the other groups. In the final reflection, the teachers noted that one image was "easier" than the other. When inquiring more about what they meant by easier, they shared that the group with the simple photo was challenged to think of as many questions as the group with a more sophisticated QFocus.

This was a bit ironic, considering they had initially chosen it because of its simplicity. The profundity of the debrief was that when it was challenging, questions came more naturally. When it was more straightforward, they exhausted their curiosity more swiftly. I couldn't have asked for a greater epiphany in terms of investigating the idea of how to spin the throttle.

HACK 11

CREATE A SAFE ZONE
ESTABLISH AN ENVIRONMENT THAT ENCOURAGES RISK-TAKING

If children feel safe, they can take risks, ask questions, make mistakes, learn to trust, share their feelings, and grow.
— ALFIE KOHN, AUTHOR AND SPEAKER

THE PROBLEM: STUDENTS DON'T TAKE LEARNING RISKS

RAPPORT. TRUST. SAFETY. These traits are fragile. They are built slowly. They can crumble quickly. They can be broken unintentionally. Nevertheless, intention matters less than perception.

The lives that children live outside of school influence how they respond inside. Some students enter with an open mind, confidence, and a genuine passion for learning. Other students' childhood experiences have given them a negative outlook on the world. They do not automatically trust adults. Yet another group of students will avoid failure at all costs. The complexities of students' experiences can make it a challenge to provide a safe environment. We might believe we have established a zone free of fear, but it is not our belief that matters.

The answer to the question you've just asked, and the lesson itself, are irrelevant if a student feels foolish or hurt for the way you've spoken to them.

Teachers do not purposefully launch questions with the intent of undermining the goal to encourage risk-taking. The reality, though, is that intent is not relevant when we are dealing with emotions. Think of the stems teachers are known to add to the beginning of a question: "Who can tell me ..." or "Raise your hand if you know ..." These qualifiers support right answers. Whether we intend to discourage risk or not, having a classroom that celebrates right answers leaves students feeling like wrong answers are evidence of failure.

So far, I have highlighted problems and suggested answers that are visible. In most cases, if you do not get the results you are seeking the first time, you have an open opportunity to reflect, tweak, and try again. This problem is different. If a teacher cannot sufficiently address this problem, they strain the effectiveness of the previous ten strategies. Without rapport, trust, and safety, all the other Hacks become uphill battles. These are feelings and emotions we are talking about now. We cannot direct students to feel comfortable. We have to use our questions and strategies to build a safe zone.

THE HACK: CREATE A SAFE ZONE

The previous ten Hacks seem more tangible than Hack 11 because the first ten answers follow a cause-and-effect sequence. Ask this question, expect this result. Building culture is less predictable and much more delicate. Antoine de Saint-Exupéry, author of *The Little Prince*, said, "A goal without a plan is just a wish." Every teacher desires to have a productive classroom where students are willing to take learning risks and be vulnerable. But we cannot wish away students feeling vulnerable in our classrooms; we have to provide the conditions that create a safe zone.

Listen to the change in the word choice. Thinking, questions, responses, and learning are terms threaded throughout every chapter leading up to now. But the culture of your environment must prioritize feelings, beliefs, trust, and rapport. We must move into different parts of the brain and deal with emotions. Emotions are powerful and often uncontrollable. Show transparency with your decisions so students are not guessing your motives. Be intentionally inclusive. Provide students with a voice so they have ownership in the classroom environment, too. Rational thinking and learning can be blocked by emotions. Ever been so angry you can't think straight? I rest my case.

Be aware of the emotions that students are exhibiting in the classroom. The answer to the question you've just asked, and the lesson itself, are irrelevant if a student feels foolish or hurt for the way you've spoken to them. This isn't a place for right answers. This is a place for all-inclusive discussions.

WHAT YOU CAN DO TOMORROW

There is no one-size-fits-all for creating a positive classroom culture. The answer is the larger idea of considering how your actions affect students emotionally and impact their willingness to be vulnerable, and maintaining that consideration as much as you can. Try these simple ideas to produce a more inviting classroom where students might be more likely to take risks.

- **Be entertained by questions.** Make up games or try one of these. Making light of questions and having fun at the same time is a win-win.

  Would You Rather

  There are always days when a lesson goes a little more quickly than planned. Take advantage of these straggling and often unproductive minutes to have a little fun with questions. Invite students to a "Would You Rather ..." query. Instead of using cards from the game, have students make up their own questions. You will accomplish three goals. 1. Students will practice asking and responding to questions with low stakes. 2. Everyone will have fun. It's nearly impossible to play this game without laughing. You have to admit, it's hysterical—in a gross sort of way—to decide if you would rather lick the bottom of a farmer's boot or chew on a rotten toenail. And 3. When students are occupied with a task, even a silly one, you are unlikely to have the behavior issues that typically surface during unstructured time.

Questions Only

The rules are simple. Two people pair up and begin asking questions of one another. You may not laugh or answer your partner's question. Hurry, if there is more than a three-second delay between questions, the last person who posed the question wins!

Twenty Questions

In this familiar game, one person secretly thinks of a subject. The opponent asks yes/no questions until guessing accurately. If necessary, the students can also use adverbs like sometimes, usually, or rarely. The winner is the person who correctly guesses the opponent's subject in the fewest number of questions.

- **Use inviting phrasing.** Most students believe it is a 100-percent commitment when they give an answer. Therefore, if they are not sure, they will avoid responding and tense up. They are either right or wrong; there is no unsure. Introduce the "maybe" for students. Permitting students

227

to under-commit allows them to save face and opens the door for them to change their minds as their understanding deepens. Simply adding "might" to a question softens it considerably. In Image 11.1, compare the questions in the absolute column to those on the right that are reworded to be more inviting.

Absolute	Inviting
• What is the author's purpose?	• What might the author's purpose be?
• What push/pull factors caused people to move westward?	• What push/pull factors might have caused people to move westward?
• What is the main idea?	• What is a possible main idea?
• Which strategy should you use?	• What strategy might work here?
• What do these systems have in common?	• What seems to be common in these two systems?
• Who knows…?	• Who is willing to share their thinking out loud?

Image 11.1

Notice that the depth of the question is not reduced. The cognitive demand can remain at the same level while increasing an approachable tone.

• **Laugh with students, not at them.** Humor is usually a way to relax an atmosphere. Enjoying a joke or laughing at something together builds memories and relationships. A sarcastic flavor of humor will not yield the same positive results. Sarcasm targets someone as a subject to mock. If a student is the focus of the joke, they might join in the giggles to hide their humiliation or embarrassment. An outward appearance that everyone is enjoying the fun can be misleading. You may be building walls you didn't plan to build.

Keep your jokes light and faceless. Be mindful of how you reference people not in the room. A student in your third-hour class will pick up on how freely you poke fun at a student from your second-hour class when that student is not there. A natural gulf might form when your third-hour student wonders what you say after the bell rings.

A joke of the day or funny story about things that you see or hear will make you an individual more than just "my teacher." Sharing a personal story about something your two-year-old said can bring a smile to anyone's face. One teacher I visited shared a corny joke of the day. These were silly puns and jokes like: *What do you call it when a giraffe swallows a jet plane? A plane in the neck.* Admit it, you smiled, didn't you?

- **Implement the 10 x 2 strategy.** This simple strategy has been shared on social media and blogs with impressive anecdotes about its power. Teachers spend two minutes a day for ten consecutive days talking to a student about anything the student wants to discuss, and then share the positive and lasting impact it had on student behavior and building rapport. Comb through your schedule and find 120 seconds you can devote to one student that day. You will be able to build quality connections with eighteen students per class over the school year.

- **Ask questions you don't know the answers to.** Transparency builds trust. Be brave enough to wonder alongside your students. That vulnerability will create safe terrain and a secure environment for students. An unwillingness to take risks in the space where you claim to embrace learning will peg you as a hypocrite. You can practice what you preach by voicing authentic questions. Who knows? Maybe a student has the answer you've been looking for.

A BLUEPRINT FOR FULL IMPLEMENTATION

Step 1: Make a list of non-negotiables for the culture you want to create in your classroom.

Consistency is one factor that builds trust. When students trust that they will not be ridiculed or dehumanized in the classroom, they begin to feel safe to step out of their comfort zone. Establishing this culture will require you to maintain certain beliefs and guarantee that they are not jeopardized. Begin by outlining the classroom you want to provide for your students. Answer these questions for yourself so you are clear on what a safe zone feels like:

- What descriptive words will define my learning space?
- How will students feel in my classroom?
- What characteristics will I model every day?
- How can I be proactive instead of reactive to potential threats to students' social and emotional safety?

Step 2: Develop a student survey and use it.

Prioritize your list of non-negotiables and seek student perspectives. Gather their feelings about the value of the descriptors you identified to see if they align. Seek their feedback on how well you are accomplishing your goals. If you use a survey like this on the first day of class, phrase the questions to access a broader scope of how they feel about school in general. Include open-ended questions that allow students to share things you might not have thought to ask, such as: How could this classroom (or school) be improved?

To build credibility with students, be transparent about the fact that their ideas matter. If a student proposes a complaint box, you might be quick to dismiss the idea to avoid a negative focus in the classroom. You can honor the suggestion by offering a suggestion box and opening it up to new ideas as well as things that might need to be changed. Be transparent about the fact that the suggestion box was a student's idea.

If other recommendations surface from your survey, be aware that this is your opportunity to show that you value their input. This does not mean that you must agree or implement every shared request. However, understanding what students feel will increase the positivity or decrease the negativity, and help you meet their needs as they see them, not exclusively how you perceive them to be.

Step 3: Co-create classroom norms with students.

When you have a clear vision of how you want students to interact with you and one another, bring your wishes to the table and invite students to share theirs, too. Developing norms is different than creating a list of rules. Norms are the way the classroom operates and how students and adults interact. They apply to everyone all the time. Rules are often expectations that are enforced as needed in regard to individuals who might break them from time to time. Rules are set by the teacher or the school's code of conduct, whereas norms are developed and agreed to as a classroom community.

Norms are co-created by everyone, and everyone is expected to adhere to them. Image 11.2 helps to clarify the difference between

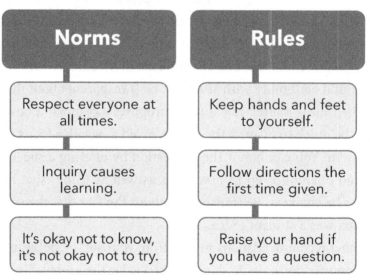

Image 11.2

rules and norms by providing a few examples. This is not a suggestion for you to adopt and use in your own classroom. Ideally, you will develop norms with your students.

Step 4: Host regular class meetings.

You can choose from several structures to set aside time in your day or week when you plan to connect with students and reflect on how things are going. Maybe it's Wednesday after music in the elementary

Class Meeting Prompts	
Goals	**Discussion Questions**
Have fun together	If a gorilla and a grizzly bear got in a fight, who would win?
School pride	What are some ways we can support our band as they go to competition this weekend?
Love learning	What is the most useful thing we learned today?
Get to know each other	If you were a superhero, what would your name be and what superpowers would you have?
Communication	What are some ways we can maintain respect and dignity when someone makes us angry?
Empathy	What might Kim need from us when she returns tomorrow after her dad's funeral?
Organization	How can we reduce the time it takes to get our materials ready for writing, so we have more time to write?
Community building	What can we do about the littering problem on campus?
Preparation	What do we need to keep in mind tomorrow when the guest teacher is here?
Teamwork	What are some potential problems that could arise in your learning teams today? How can we avoid them?
Goal setting	What do you plan to accomplish today? How will you meet that goal? How can we help one another?

Image 11.3

grades. For secondary teachers, you might set aside the first Friday of the month. Whatever the frequency, stick with it. Consistency and predictability will provide a sense of comfort for many students.

This is a time to listen. Some teachers have an open dialogue and ask students to share what's on their minds. Another approach is to offer a question to prompt discussion. Consider what you might be able to achieve as a result of your class meeting, and select a question accordingly. The table in Image 11.3 provides a selection of topics and one example to get you thinking.

Keep the tone positive and productive. It's beneficial to have the structure in place to discuss problems within the classroom, but the goal is to open communication of all kinds, not to fixate on negativity. If you find yourself running short on time, choose a quick prompt, rather than skip a scheduled class meeting. Keeping your precious time with them will be evidence that your classroom culture is a priority.

Step 5: Use validation rather than rational thinking when faced with an emotional mind.

People—not just school-aged children, but adults too—are temporarily unable to think or even listen to reason when their emotions flare. Do not confuse this with a lack of logical ideas or solutions. Think of it as a wall of emotions that blocks the person's access to logic and reasoning. The logic and reason are in there, they are just barricaded by fear, worry, frustration, or embarrassment. If your head is thinking a student's emotions are unjustified, exaggerated, unsubstantiated, or borderline irrational, that's when step five keeps your zone a safe place.

When emotions get high, your gut will tell you to solve the problem and do it as fast as you can. As a teacher, your natural instinct is to grab a teachable moment and attempt to defuse the student's emotions. You might even say something like, "It's not a big deal" or even more directly, "Calm down." Then it gets worse. Both of those responses come from your rational state of mind.

Rational thinking and emotional minds do not mix well. I don't mean the oil-and-water kind of not mixing. I mean the gasoline-and-fire kind. To soothe these emotions, validate them. Rather than dismissing or discrediting frustration, acknowledge it. When someone tells you that something shouldn't bother you, does that annoyance disappear? Not usually. Oftentimes, it escalates. Image 11.4 illustrates how to validate in lieu of using logic when a student is not ready to hear your advice.

Emotional Statement	Rational Response	Validation
She's talking behind my back!	So? It's not hurting you.	You are really worried about what she is saying.
He won't let me play!	Find someone else to hang out with.	It feels really crummy to be left out.
You're always picking on me!	Always, huh? What about yesterday when…	Sounds like you feel targeted today.
I always have to do all the work!	If you would have just…	I'm guessing you're frustrated with your group's productivity.
I don't know what to do about this situation!	What if you…	It's hard when you're not sure what decision to make.
I'll never get this done!	Then I guess you better get started now.	It can be stressful when you are short on time.

Image 11.4

You will notice the student calming as you validate consecutively. When the emotional mind is diffused, the barriers go away, and you will be able to use your problem-solving techniques to help the student resolve the issue. But beware! If your emotional radar is off, you will be back to square one in no time flat. A conservative approach is to follow a validating statement with a question about the student's state of mind. Try something like, "Looks like you're calming down. Are you ready to talk about what comes next?" Don't be surprised if your offer is declined. Remember, the issue isn't that the student does not know how to solve the problem. The issue is that the emotions are in the way. After you remove the barrier of fear, anger, or frustration, the student is ready to access their own logical thinking. Seems like magic—and it kind of is.

Step 6: Deliberately build and protect trust.

When my son was younger, he went through a period when telling the truth was not his default response. My husband and I tried everything to prevent him from lying to us. Sometimes he would make up stories for what seemed like no reason at all. To illustrate the fragility of trust, we told him to fill a pitcher with water one tablespoon at a time. The pitcher represented how much trust he had earned back after being untruthful. The water represented one occasion of keeping his word, showing responsibility, or telling the truth. He held the measuring spoon under the faucet. When it was full, he carefully walked it down the counter toward the pitcher. He labeled each spoonful with something he was going to do to earn trust.

The point of the exercise was not to brainstorm two hundred ways to build trust. The lesson was that earning trust is a slow process. One breach and your entire pitcher tips, forcing you to start all over again. Every ten or fifteen tablespoons he filled, my husband and I would label an act that broke trust and empty the pitcher into the sink. After what probably seemed like a lifetime of walking up and down our kitchen, our son would hold on to the pitcher and plead with us not to dump it out.

That young boy is now a United States Marine. The Corps Values are honor, courage, and commitment. Honor includes filling the pitcher and keeping it full. The pitcher does not fill itself. It takes transparent and repetitive actions that show your character. It is the same when you are earning a student's trust. One relationship at a time, you show your trustworthiness through predictable behaviors that honor student dignity at all times. Many of these relationships are fragile. A sarcastic comment at a student's expense might not only empty your pitcher, but put a hole in the bottom that can't be plugged.

OVERCOMING PUSHBACK

Sometimes it feels like there is always one more thing for teachers to consider on top of teaching the content. When relationships are placed in the "one more thing" bucket, they perceive that building them is optional. It isn't.

I have so much content to teach, I simply don't have time to build a culture. You don't have time *not* to. First of all, working in a tense environment day after day is not good for you. Coming to school to enjoy spending the day with your students makes life happier for everyone. In addition, a positive rapport prevents wasted time redirecting and negotiating with students who do not feel safe or don't enjoy school.

Some kids can't be reached, no matter how hard you try. This belief comes from a fixed mindset of someone who has already given up on a student. Some students take longer to respond to efforts to build rapport. Consistency is a key piece of establishing trust. The one who measures when your behavior is consistent enough to be predictable is the student. In most cases, students transfer to you the relationships that they have had with people before they met you. The willingness to take risks might be immediate with students who have had multiple positive experiences with their emotional safety. Students who have had unpredictable or hurtful adults in their lives will be much slower to let their guard down with you.

Students won't take this seriously. Sometimes, a little silliness is just what we need. Forcing students to have fun is an oxymoron. Hesitation to get involved in the fun might be a sign of discomfort, not noncompliance. When it comes to lightening the mood to enjoy laughs with students, it is counterproductive to get into a spitting contest about whether or not the student will participate. This might be a time when a student can choose to observe.

When students are emotional, I don't always have time to speak to them one-on-one. Your relationship with a student will grow if you find time to have a quiet conversation. In cases when time just doesn't allow it, you are better off not asking questions. Positive statements are less likely to trigger emotions or draw you into the conversation before you can set aside time and space to give the student your full attention.

The following comments offer an upbeat message with a low probability of opening a can of worms:

- I'm glad you're here today.

- I hope your day is fantastic.

- Looking forward to seeing you tomorrow.

- Thanks for being here.

- Good morning, (name).

THE HACK IN ACTION

Rome wasn't built in a day, and culture isn't developed in a class period. After visiting Mrs. Barbara Silkes in her third-grade classroom at Cornwell Avenue School, I was eager to hear how she created such a safe yet academically challenging environment. The eight- to nine-year-olds in her classroom spoke to one another like young professionals. Mutual respect and genuine empathy were the norms.

There is not a book to share or a poster to hang that builds the kind of environment where students feel valued, and in return, they value education. On the day I observed Mrs. Silkes, the lesson was a shared reading of the book *Amazing Grace* by Mary Hoffman. The story is about a young girl who wants to be Peter Pan in the school play. One character tells Grace she can't be Peter Pan because that's a boy's name. Another points out that she can't play the part because Peter Pan isn't black. As Mrs. Silkes maneuvered through the story, she tackled the realities of prejudice and discrimination. The third-graders expressed empathy, respect, comfort, and compassion. They spoke and listened to one another in a class discussion that Mrs. Silkes activated, but which came from her students' hearts. It was evident that the students trusted in her and in each other. Clearly, the students felt socially and academically safe.

When I asked Mrs. Silkes how she was able to establish this culture in the fall of the year, she was eager and ready to share the non-negotiables that she strives to achieve.

She identified these nine components that she mindfully considers to ensure her students feel safe to take risks in her room:

1. I model **consistency**. My behavior, demeanor, reactions, personality, and the teacher they see are predictable and dependable.

2. This consistency develops **trust and safety**. Students should never, ever feel "on edge." School should be their safety zone.

3. I strive to be **responsive** rather than reactive to behavioral issues that arise.

4. I nurture classroom **unity** by creating a family environment where we protect one another, are loyal to one another, and care for and respect one another in the classroom, during recess, and even at the bus stop. From September to June, we are one family.

5. I create family **connections** outside the classroom by making frequent phone calls, having face-to-face meetings, communicating through ClassDojo each and every day, including weekends, and sometimes even paying a visit to a home if need be. The connections created are solid and the families and students realize I'm their educational advocate for the year.

6. I model **patience** by being patient, and expecting patience in return.

7. I show my students **unconditional acceptance** of their strengths and challenges and frequently remind

them that we are all works in progress and that being "fair" may not look "equal."

8. I model **transparency, honesty, and fallibility** by admitting to mistakes I've made, maintaining a sense of humor about myself, and communicating the fact that it's really okay not to be perfect— because none of us are.

9. My students begin and end each day **knowing I truly care about them.**

Mrs. Silkes was prepared to share her plan for fostering an accepting learning environment. She set a vision for how students would feel in her classroom, then deliberately implemented steps to make it a reality.

From the onset of the development of this book, I knew Hack 11 was the most important one. Throughout my entire writing process, it was sequenced as Hack 1. It was obvious to me that a classroom culture will make or break a teacher's ability to leverage the power of questioning to create an inquiry-based classroom. Therefore, it was logical that the stage should be set up front. As the book evolved, I moved Create a Safe Zone from Hack 1 to Hack 11. It felt hypocritical of Hack 3 not to punctuate your reading with the significance of culture.

I spent hours on this idea of reflection and analysis of teachers who connect with students. How can we bottle up and share what some teachers naturally have? We all want to experience the magic that happens when students and teachers have rapport, trust, and safety. There is no copy/paste way to guarantee a culture of inquiry in your classroom. On the other hand, there is a way to guarantee that inquiry is not appreciated and cultivated. That is to give no merit to Hack 11.

In his book, *Visible Learning for Teachers: Maximizing Impact on Learning,* Professor John Hattie identifies four components to how teachers establish credibility. Trust, dynamism, competence, and immediacy are equally important in determining how credible students deem you to be. The eleven Hacks shared in this text give the most recognition to competence and immediacy. Dynamism is addressed by energizing a passion for questioning. Hack 11 stands alone to establish trust. With it, you will multiply your success in the other ten Hacks.

CONCLUSION
AN EXERCISE

PUT DOWN YOUR writing utensil. Before writing your responses, take yourself back to think about your **greatest** year, with your **favorite** class, on your **best** day. If you are a new teacher, imagine what it will be like.

Got it?

If you're smiling, you are ready to read on.

Still thinking about your greatest/favorite/best, read the following questions. When your thoughts are clear, write down your answers.

1. What was your purpose for asking questions?

2. For what reasons did students ask questions?

As you thought about the intentions you and your students had for questions, consider what conditions existed to support those beliefs. For most teachers, their list includes a combination of content or academic focus and emotions that connect to fond memories of relationships, even a sense of family.

Now fast forward to today. How close is your everyday classroom aligned with your greatest/favorite/best? If you were to ask your students why you ask questions and what reasons they ask questions, would their perceptions align with yours? Why or why not?

Are students actively questioning themselves to support their own learning, or do they only ask questions they expect you to answer? Who or what is the source of information in the classroom? Is it you? Should it be? Why or why not?

When students struggle, to what causes do you attribute it? Are you approaching the challenge with a growth mindset? How would you know if a fixed mindset is creeping in to excuse you from asking the tough questions?

Do you model reflection? What role does it play in your own growth? What learning goals do you have for yourself? Are you on track for achieving them? What is causing you to be on/off-track? What strategies do you have to support yourself in reaching these goals? What will success look like?

What Hacks will you create on your own to cultivate a classroom of inquiry? Teaching and learning do not rest in a single category of facts and answers. Sometimes the "answers" lie in searching for the right questions.

Teaching is complex. If it were a matter of simply applying a formula for inspiring learning, teachers would be replaced with robots that are programmed not to deviate from the code. Tone, delivery, and relationships impact the quality, rate, and depth of learning. The reward in teaching parallels the joy we aim for our students to feel about learning. It's challenging, but it's worth it.

As Albert Einstein said, "The important thing is not to stop questioning."

APPENDIX

I N THIS SECTION, I define the protocols referenced throughout *Hacking Questions*, with additional exercises for you to consider as you implement them. Please visit hackingquestions.com for easy-to-download, copy-ready templates and printable posters to help you put these Hacks into action.

GROUPING

This list of strategies for grouping students offers a variety of approaches. Some allow you to access predetermined partners when needed, and others give the perception to students that they are randomly assigned, even if they are not. There are even options for those times when you see a need in the moment to give students a verbal think.

Clock Partners. Each student has an image of a clock on a sheet of paper they keep in their desk or folder. Assign "appointments" for students with other students in the class. Preselecting partners allows you to quickly and routinely change up the partners in the classroom, without wasting time assigning a partner or dealing with the odd man out. Younger students can have as few as three appointments, with the option to change them when needed. Older students or larger classrooms have the option to make as many as twelve appointments. A schedule for switching the appointments is up to you. Because the Clock Partners are rarely table partners or elbow partners, it also offers a short and manageable opportunity to embed a controlled movement in the classroom to keep students alert and their brain juices flowing.

Some teachers are systematic in how they use Clock Partners. For example, the 12 o'clock partner is a student with a similar reading level. The 3 o'clock partner is a friend or someone the student is comfortable talking to. The 6 o'clock partner is a peer with a similar social level. Quieter students are partnered with quieter students and more vocal students can partner with peers who are equally talkative. The 9 o'clock partners come from mismatched levels, where low-achieving students are paired with medium-level learners, and medium-levels are paired with high achievers. (A download is available at hackingquestions.com.)

Elbow Partners. Wherever students are seated, they partner up with a person close to their elbow. This works well on the carpet or at tables.

Face Partners. When seated, students have a conversation with the person they see when they look straight ahead. When your room is arranged in groups, but you want them only to speak to one person rather than the whole table, this is a good option.

Musical Shares. Use music to encourage students to move around the room. When the music stops, they partner up with the closest person.

Stand Up-Hand Up-Pair Up. Students stand up and mingle until the teacher gives the cue to put their hands up. At that time, they pair up with the closest hand. When they find a partner, they put their hands down. This makes it easy to see who is still not partnered up.

Think-Pair-Square. After you pose a question, give students time to think and organize their thoughts around the question. After sufficient think time (five to thirty seconds, depending on the complexity of the question), give individuals the opportunity to share their thoughts with another person. Instead of the traditional whole-class share-out, try joining pairs of students to form a group of four—or a square—to compare the thinking of each person in the group. Be purposeful with where you position yourself during this peer conversation. This is an ideal time to listen to specific students to get a quick check on where they are in their learning process.

Three (or Four) of a Kind. Use an old deck of playing cards and distribute one to each student. You can be intentional with the cards you assign or make it random. Save yourself time and greet students as they enter the classroom with a "Hello, here's your card." It will give them a little heads up that you have something different planned. Have students organize themselves according to those cards—all the fours in one group, all the aces in one group. As an added bonus, playing cards allow you to quickly sort in two different ways. After they've done their three (or four) of a kind group, have them reshuffle, find a suit partner, and make a mini flush.

ALL HANDS UP

These strategies are good replacements for the traditional format of ping-pong questioning. The intent is for all students to have the opportunity to cognitively engage and make their thinking visible.

Ask-Ask-Trade. Provide a question or fact to each student and ask them to find a partner. The first partner asks the second partner to respond to the question or provide information about the fact. Next, the second partner does the same. After both partners have discussed their questions or facts, they trade questions and find new partners. This is particularly helpful for vocabulary, math facts, or world language classes.

Back-to-Back and Face-to-Face. With a partner, students stand back-to-back so they cannot see their partner. Pose a question to the entire class and give them sufficient think time. During the think time, make sure they stay with their backs turned to each other. When you give the signal (a direction or a sound), the students can turn around to face their partners and discuss the prompt. After a given time (forty-five to ninety seconds is often a good start) have them turn back-to-back again, and stop talking. Then read the next prompt. You may modify this protocol by switching partners between each question.

Choral Response. This protocol works best for short and succinct answers. Hold your hands up with palms facing out. Pose a question and keep your hands up, giving every student sufficient think time. Then drop your hands and flip your palms up. When your hands reach the bottom of their descent, students respond in unison.

Pick It-Show It. Give students index cards, flash cards, or pieces of paper with possible responses. When you pose a question, have each student select the one that matches their thinking. Students can display their cards silently, then communicate to a peer why they chose that card. You can also implement response cards with partners. Each pair of students only receives one set of cards. Partner A chooses the correct response and explains why to Partner B. Then Partner B finds a Partner A from another team and compares Team One's thinking to Team Two's thinking.

Write It-Show It. Provide students with KleenSlates, chalkboards, or blank sheets of paper. When you pose a question, have students write their response in words, pictures, or diagrams. This quick and low-stress routine affords all students an opportunity to participate in the process of recall. There is a significant difference in what happens in a student's mind when they're asked to remember and say a word, rather than listen to another person in the room repeat a word. Students are more likely to retrieve the language they need when applying their learning and having dialogic conversations. It also serves as a quick check to determine whether students are connecting the dots or if they require more practice.

MOVEMENT

Movement keeps the blood pumping and the brain active. Students who do not like to be on the spot are more likely to engage when they're moving, because sitting in their seats attracts attention. Getting students up and around encourages blood flow and increases oxygen to the brain, and both are helpful when we want students to be at their best for learning.

Four Corners. Label parts of the room with possible responses to your question, such as A/B/C/D, strongly agree/agree/strongly disagree/disagree, or always/sometimes/rarely/never. After posing a question, invite students to gather in the part of the room that corresponds with their thinking. There, they can have a standing conversation with others who have similar points of view. An optional twist on this protocol is to pair students from one side of the room with students from another to hear different points of view.

Gallery Walk. Individually or in small groups, have students create a visual to show their learning or explain an idea. Invite them to rotate around the room and visit the different learning exhibits. You can vary the gallery walk in many ways. Options include allowing students to roam and visit the pieces they choose rather than a systematic rotation. Determine whether you want the visuals to stand alone or if one person from the group will stay behind to give a short synopsis and answer questions for the visitors.

Human Graph. Instead of simply standing in place, ask the students to form a line to represent a bar graph. The visual allows students to compare responses and have discussions with students who agree or disagree with them.

Standing Poll. When a question is asked, tell students to stand when they agree with a response. They can pair up with others who share their same point of view or compare thinking with someone who stood for a different response. For a variation, ask all the students to begin standing up. Pose the question and embed think time by allowing them to sit down when they have clarity.

WRITING

Sometimes it is necessary to create a hard copy of student thoughts, especially when you want to use the responses to differentiate students or intentionally group them in the future, based on what they know and don't yet know. These protocols also pair nicely with many of the talk protocols. When they are done individually, you will see the effectiveness of the collaboration time by collecting data on what each student is taking away.

Make an Analogy. Provide a sentence stem for students to compare your learning concept to something else, and have them explain why they made the comparison. This not only sparks creativity and gives you insight into the depth of their understanding, but it can also be fun, and sometimes adds humor to the lesson. Example: (Provide the concept) is like _____ because ...

Student examples:

- Lower elementary: Reading is like brushing your teeth because you have to do it every day.

- Upper elementary: Martin Luther King is like a bumblebee because he pollinates his message from person to person, no matter what color they are.

- Middle school: Multiplying two negative numbers is like saying, "I don't have no money." Because if you don't have none, you must have some.

- High school: Stalin is like the tin man because he was heartless.

Numbered Word Summary. When chunking larger pieces of information or processing complex ideas, task students with summarizing it. Limit the number of words they may use in their summary to no more than six. When identifying a big idea, you can even ask students to limit it to a one-word summary. A supportive modification for students who need it is to allow them to write their complete summary first, then underline the number of words from their summary that are most important.

Stop and Jot. Have students stop and use a journal, whiteboard, or laptop to write down key points they are learning and to document any questions they have. When students think and write about their learning, they are more likely to retain the information and use it to make connections later.

Three-Two-One. Bring students' attention to what they're learning, how they're learning it, and where they will go next with a Three-Two-One. Three things I have learned, two ways I supported my learning, and one question I still have. (A template is available at hackingquestions.com.)

BRAINSTORMING

When it is time to generate ideas, these strategies will do the trick. The brainstorming protocols will give students the opportunity to see the benefits of collaborating with peers. The underlying theme in all these protocols is that multiple heads are better than one.

Affinity Mapping. To help students organize a list of thoughts or ideas, use this categorization structure. Each idea is written on a separate sticky note. It is important not to put more than one on each note. After the group has collected all their thoughts, they group the sticky notes that are similar together. Do not provide students with names for the categories. They will determine the most appropriate label for the groups they developed. This helps students differentiate bigger ideas from smaller ones.

Brain Dump. To prepare for conversations, have students activate schema with a brain dump. When given a learning focus, ask students to write everything they can think of that relates to that topic. Use a brain dump to search for prior knowledge they bring to the lesson, or to help them recall information from a previous lesson to refresh their memories.

Chalk Talk. On a single sheet of large paper, have students brainstorm ideas based on a provided prompt or question. Ask them to communicate only in writing on the chart paper. Writing instead of talking gives everybody an equal voice.

Give One-Get One. Ask students to brainstorm ideas individually. Document the information on a grid you provide on a sheet of paper. Students should fill in as many boxes as they can, then approach other classmates, give them an idea, and get one idea. The learners continue to give and get ideas until their grids are complete.

See-Think-Wonder. Slow students down and ask them to look closely at a visual or piece of text. Separate their thinking processes by asking them to notice, first. What do you see? Then reflect on what predictions or assumptions that observation leads to. Finally, encourage students to wonder beyond what is explicitly provided by the author or artist.

DISCUSSION

Use these protocols when you want students to have conversations about their learning. The discussion protocols typically work best after learning. However, they can be used at any time during a lesson to encourage student collaboration.

Fan and Pick. Write questions related to your lesson on index cards and organize students in groups of four. Student One fans the questions out for Student Two to choose one. The card selected by Student Two is read to Student Three, who responds or solves the problem. Student Four responds by paraphrasing Student Three's response or providing feedback. The roles are rotated, and the process is repeated. The questions on the cards can be supplied for students or written by students.

Fiction Detection. Students write three statements related to key ideas in their learning. Two of the statements will be true while one will be false. In small groups, students take turns reading their three statements. The other students in the group individually try to detect which statement is fiction. They can write the number on a sheet of paper or a KleenSlate, and show it to their group.

Final Word. Highlight key points in a lesson and allow for multiple perspectives with this protocol. Each group member chooses three quotes from the text. Individually, the students reflect on their chosen quotes and prioritize them from first to last. The criteria for prioritizing can vary, such as key points, most resonating, or the biggest *aha*. The first student shares the quote without any explanation. The other students discuss the quote while the first student only listens. Set a timer for their dialogue. When the timer goes off, the first student gets the baton again. At this point, the student shares why they chose the quote and responds to the comments made by the other group members. Repeat the process until every student gets a final word.

Hot Shot in a Hot Spot. When learning progress is stalled, this strategy can help pick up the speed. Determine hot shots who have a sound understanding of a lesson or parts of the lesson. A student with extra background knowledge or special experiences can also be a hot shot. Position those students in different locations in the room. These are your hot spots. The rest of the class identifies the information they need and which hot spot can provide it. The learners gather around a hot spot to learn from one of their hot shot peers.

Rinse and Repeat. This is intended to be short and sweet. Each student on a team takes a turn to quickly share comments about the learning. No cross talk is allowed. Each student should be succinct in their shared thoughts. Use this to check for understanding and summarize learning so far, within a lesson or as a lesson closure.

Stir the Class. Start students in groups of three to five. Assign a number to each student within the group and provide a discussion topic related to your lesson. After students have had sufficient time to discuss the topic, announce a number. The student assigned to that number rotates to a new group and summarizes Group One's thinking to Group Two. This person is now a member of the second group. Pose another discussion item for groups to discuss, and repeat the sequence, choosing another random student number to rotate. To change it up, use a die or a spinner to choose the student number selected to move to a new group.

Triad. Assign three partners as A, B, and C. Prepare three or six open-ended questions that will cause students to reflect or give extended responses. Each question is one round. In the first round, Partner A responds to the inquiry, Partner B uses active listening skills for questioning and paraphrasing to keep the conversation going, and Partner C observes, listens, and takes notes. After a specified period of time (start with two minutes and work up/down from there), stop the conversation between Partners A and B. Turn the floor to Partner C to summarize what was heard. Give Partner C half the time that Partners A and B had to talk. In round two, a new inquiry is shared and the roles are rotated. The final rotation happens in round three to provide everyone with an opportunity to serve in each role. Do one or two complete rotations of three rounds depending on the number of questions you want them to discuss.

Turn and Ask. Instead of turning and talking to your partner, remind students to begin their dialogue with a question. When the first partner asks, this guarantees that each person has an opportunity to say something, even if it was just posing the question.

Word. Phrase. Sentence. Determine the size of the collaborative groups. This protocol works best with smaller groups of two to four. Each student chooses a word, phrase, and sentence that resonates with them and is related to the learning. One at a time, each student shares their word, followed by a group discussion about all the words shared. Next, students share their selected phrase one at a time. Again, follow with a group discussion. Finally, the learners share their sentences with or without cross talk between each share.

TEMPLATES, RESOURCES, AND POSTERS

You will find the following items available for download at hackingquestions.com:

Templates and Resources

- Three-Two-One
- Clock Partners
- Exit Ticket
- Fan and Pick Assignments
- Four Corners Labels
- Give One-Get One

- In Your Pocket Questions
- Pick It-Show It Options
- QKAN
- Reciprocal Teaching Questions
- Triad Directions
- Word Sentence Phrase

Posters

- ABC: Agree, Build, Challenge
- Instead of IDK Choices
- Pinball Talk Moves
- Punctuate Your Learning
- Qualify Your Response

- Question-Answer Relationship Definitions
- Scaffold Sequence: Question, Prompt, Cue
- Tomorrow's Help Scale
- What Active Listeners Do

More from
TIMES 10

Browse all titles at 10Publications.com

Hacking School Discipline
9 Ways to Create a Culture of Empathy & Responsibility Using Restorative Justice
By Nathan Maynard and Brad Weinstein

Reviewers proclaim this *Washington Post* Bestseller to be "maybe the most important book a teacher can read, a must for all educators, fabulous, a game changer!" Teachers and presenters Nathan Maynard and Brad Weinstein demonstrate how to eliminate punishment and build a culture of responsible students and independent learners in a book that will become your new blueprint for school discipline. Eighteen straight months at #1 on Amazon and still going strong, *Hacking School Discipline* is disrupting education like nothing we've seen in decades—maybe centuries.

Hacking Classroom Management
10 Ideas To Help You Become the Type of Teacher They Make Movies About
By Mike Roberts

Learn the ten ideas you can use today to create the classroom any great movie teacher would love. Utah English Teacher of the Year and sought-after speaker Mike Roberts brings you quick and easy classroom management Hacks that will make your classroom the place to be for all your students. He shows you how to create an amazing learning environment that makes discipline, rules, and consequences obsolete, no matter if you're a new teacher or a thirty-year veteran teacher.

Browse all titles at 10Publications.com

Hacking Engagement
50 Tips & Tools to Engage Teachers and Learners Daily
By James Alan Sturtevant

If you're a teacher who appreciates quick ideas to engage your students, this is the book for you. *Hacking Engagement* provides fifty unique, exciting, and actionable tips and tools that you can apply right now. Try one of these amazing engagement strategies tomorrow: engage the enraged, create celebrity couple nicknames, hash out a hashtag, avoid the war on yoga pants, let your freak flag fly, become a proponent of the exponent, and transform your class into a focus group. Are you ready to engage?

Hacking Education
10 Quick Fixes For Every School
By Mark Barnes and Jennifer Gonzalez

In this award-winning first Hack Learning Series book, Mark Barnes and Jennifer Gonzalez employ decades of teaching experience and hundreds of discussions with education thought leaders to show you how to find and hone the quick fixes that every school and classroom need. Using a hacker's mentality, they provide one aha moment after another with ten quick fixes for every school—solutions to everyday problems and teaching methods that any teacher or administrator can implement immediately.

Browse all titles at 10Publications.com

Hacking Project Based Learning

10 Easy Steps to PBL and Inquiry in the Classroom

By Ross Cooper and Erin Murphy

As questions and mysteries around PBL and inquiry continue to swirl, experienced classroom teachers and school administrators Ross Cooper and Erin Murphy empower those intimidated by PBL to cry, "I can do this!" while providing added value for those who are already familiar with the process. *Hacking Project Based Learning* demystifies what PBL is all about with ten Hacks that construct a simple path that educators and students can easily follow to achieve success.

Project Based Learning

Real Questions. Real Answers. How to Unpack PBL and Inquiry

By Ross Cooper and Erin Murphy

Educators would love to leverage project based learning to create learner-centered opportunities for their students, but why isn't PBL the norm? Because teachers have questions. *Project Based Learning* is Ross Cooper and Erin Murphy's response to the most common and complex questions educators ask about PBL and inquiry, including: How do I structure a PBL experience? How do I get grades? How do I include direct instruction? What happens when kids don't work well together? Learn how to teach with PBL and inquiry in any subject or grade.

Browse all titles at 10Publications.com

Resources from Times 10

Nurture your inner educator:
10publications.com/educatortype

Podcasts:
hacklearningpodcast.com
jamesalansturtevant.com/podcast

On Twitter:
@10Publications
@HackMyLearning
#Times10News
#RealPBL
@LeadForward2
#LeadForward
#HackLearning
#HackingLeadership
#MakeWriting
#HackingQs
#HackingSchoolDiscipline
#LeadWithGrace
#QuietKidsCount
#ModernMentor
#AnxiousBook
#QuitPoint

All things Times 10:
10publications.com

ABOUT THE AUTHOR

Connie Hamilton is a two-time Hack Learning Series author. In 2016, she co-authored *Hacking Homework* with Starr Sackstein. Connie has dedicated nearly twenty-five years to the field of education, and has served her profession as a teacher, instructional coach, principal, and district curriculum director. Connie achieved her Educational Specialist from Oakland University in educational leadership. She earned her Master of Arts degree in educational administration, with an emphasis on curriculum and instruction, from Central Michigan University. Her Spartan pride was cultivated when she obtained her Bachelor of Arts degree in education.

She is serving her fourteenth year at Saranac Community Schools in Saranac, Michigan, and is now the part-time district curriculum director. Connie spends most of her remaining time consulting with schools. She shares her experience and knowledge by providing engaging professional learning workshops and following up to support the implementation of instructional strategies in the classroom. As a workshop presenter, Connie has traveled to multiple states and throughout Canada. She concentrates on instructional strategies, with a passion for questioning. Participants attending her events describe them as relevant, engaging, and worthwhile.

Connie currently lives near Grand Rapids, Michigan, with her husband, Paul. They have three children. Trey (Paul III) is an illustration student at the College for Creative Studies. Luke is an active duty Private in the United States Marine Corps. Allie is a high school junior planning a career as an autism consultant.

Follow Connie Hamilton on Twitter at @conniehamilton and use the hashtag #HackingQs.

Email her at conniehamilton12@gmail.com. Visit her webpages at www.conniehamilton.org and www.hackingquestions.com.

ACKNOWLEDGMENTS

I WANT TO EXPRESS my appreciation to the teachers highlighted in *Hacking Questions*. It is inspiring to witness your willingness to model vulnerability and continuous learning. Thank you for sharing your successes with the world of education.

Mrs. Barb Aguirre, middle school ELA

Mr. Dean Bourazeris, middle school social studies

Mrs. Elizabeth Brownwell, middle school ELA

Mrs. Kate Budzinski, fourth grade

Ms. Annette Buttle, second grade

Mrs. Barbara Cizauskas, kindergarten

Ms. Jennifer A. Corrado, second grade

Mrs. Maureen Jorgensen, third grade

Mrs. Amy Miles, middle school science

Mrs. Michelle Perkins, fifth grade

Mrs. Barbara Silkes, third grade

Ms. Laura Sloma, high school physics

Mrs. Mary Steinberg, high school, math

Mrs. Paula Warren, high school ELA

This book would not be possible without the commitment to teaching and learning made by school districts and their leaders who participated in the Collaborative and Instructional Feedback Teams (CIFTs).

Center Line Public Schools, Lisa Oleski

Detroit Public Schools, Kristen Maher

Kentwood Public Schools, Evan Hordyk
Linden Community Schools, Brett Young
Saranac Community Schools, Jason Smith
Soledad Unified School District, Dianne Witwer
Southgate Community Schools, Michelle Baker-Herring
Trenton Public Schools, Ann Deneroff
West Hempstead Union Free School District, Dina Reilly

TIMES 10 provides practical solutions that busy educators can read today and use tomorrow. We bring you content from experienced teachers and leaders, and we share it through books, podcasts, webinars, articles, events, and ongoing conversations on social media. Our books and materials help turn practice into action. Stay in touch with us at 10Publications.com and follow our updates on Twitter @10Publications and #Times10News.

Made in the USA
Las Vegas, NV
13 July 2021